# LAWS IMPARTING RURAL DEVELOPMENT IN INDIA



PRASOON KUMAR MISHRA

Made with ♥ on the Notion Press Platform
www.notionpress.com

I DEDICATE THIS BOOK TO...

My Parents who are my real God, My brothers, Sisters & Relatives

Who are my Emotional Strength,

My wife who is my Soul Mate And my dear Son.

# Contents

Contents

# Contents

# Preface

The journey of writing this book starts with the concept of development of India in true sense with the development of Rural Nation and how the laws of this country plays a role in this regard.

This book is divided into many parts with subheadings and descriptions which have distinctive subject area

The representation in the form of this book is nothing but a collection of different laws and Supreme Court judgments which shows relation of laws with Rural Development.

The author will feel obliged for tendering constructive suggestions from any quarters for the improvement of the book in onward editions. The author hopes that the book will serve the need of readers who are working in the field of village development and the person interested in this area. With good wish to all my readers for their progressive professional step ahead.

Delhi: 12-10-2024 Prasoon Kumar Mishra

CHAPTER ONE

# INTRODUCTION

As per the Planning Commission of India (PCI), rural meaning refers to the geographical area where the maximum population of Indians is 15,000. In addition, it can also be an area where the population density remains 400 people per square kilometer. According to the Population Census of 2011, the percentage of people residing in rural areas is close to 69% of the Indian population. It roughly about 83.3 crore Indians who are settled in rural areas. As per another report by the Government of India, the percentage of the Indian population that was situated Below the Poverty Line (BPL) in 2011-2012 amounted to 21.9%. Thus, rural development also includes the measures implemented by government bodies to curb the poverty rate in such areas. Therefore, the objectives of rural development include providing opportunities for earning a respectable livelihood. Consequently, the rural population will be able to relieve themselves of poverty and economic backwardness. The policy-makers in India attempt to introduce modern education, health standards, and land reforms to offer the rural inhabitants a standard of living. In this way Rural development in India is the overall progress in the economic and social conditions of Indians residing in rural areas.

For that, the rural population requires long-lasting reforms and consistent projects on rural development in India in sectors such as agriculture, education, and health. With necessary steps and measures, it is thus possible to introduce development in rural landmasses that will stand the test of time. The primary objectives of rural development include the following –

i) To promote economic growth among the rural population through adequate access to food, shelter, clothing, education, and employment. With proper opportunities proportional to the same in urban areas, individuals residing in rural areas will be able to get a level ground for income options.

ii) To introduce modern techniques for agriculture in rural areas to contribute to an increased productivity. The role of rural development is to establish sustainable and affordable technology to increase production in a national market.

iii) To ensure consistent rural infrastructure development in India. In addition, this process should involve all local rural populations. Consequently, they will gain the agency to make large-scale economic decisions that lead to area-based financial development.

iv) To bridge the gap between local governing bodies and the Central administration for better economic development and for that, rural development aims to provide executive powers to panchayats for carrying on the policies framed by experts.

v) Finally, the objective of rural development is to use natural resources within a territory to ensure maximum economic benefit for inhabitants. This also includes important land reform measures to boost the agricultural output and productivity of every individual involved.

How to Ensure the Rural Development of India?

The Government of India has launched multiple projects on rural development in India over the decades. The keys to sustainable rural development in terms of economic situation include the following –

i) Proper presence of advanced facilities for irrigation to all land types in India. As a result, farmers can boost their agricultural output and create economic opportunities for themselves.

ii) Credit facilities on access to the necessary ingredients of farming such as fertilizers, pesticides, and seeds. Subsidies on electricity used for farming purposes ensure that the rural population saves more than it spends.

iii) Combat with social inequalities and discrimination in rural areas to create a sense of unity. This sense of social unity will lead to the formation of an economic class whose aim is to boost production and ensure rural development.

iv) Make sure that there are adequate training sessions for farmers to equip them with modern agricultural measures. Besides, farmers should also be aware of agricultural policies, land reforms, and market prices for the best use of their resources.

In addition, any improvement in current agricultural markets also makes sure that they can accommodate the economic contribution of the rural population. In these ways, one can ensure a sustainable growth curve and desirable rural development of India.

GOAL AND OBJECTIVES

Studying law for rural development can have several objectives, including:

i) Legal Empowerment: To empower rural communities by providing them with legal knowledge and tools to protect their rights and interests.

Access to Justice: To ensure that rural populations have access to the legal system and can seek redress for issues like land disputes, property rights, and social justice.

ii) Sustainable Development: To promote laws and policies that support sustainable and equitable development in rural areas, such as land reform, environmental protection, and social welfare.

iii) Poverty Alleviation: To address legal issues that affect poverty in rural areas, including access to healthcare, education, and economic opportunities.

Social Justice: To work towards a more just and equal society, addressing issues like gender equality, discrimination, and the rights of marginalized communities in rural areas.

iv) Policy Advocacy: To engage in policy advocacy and legal reform to create an enabling environment for rural development.

v) Conflict Resolution: To help resolve conflicts and disputes in rural communities through legal mechanisms.

vi) Land Rights: To protect and strengthen the land rights of rural populations, which is often a crucial aspect of rural development.

vii) Capacity Building: To build the legal capacity of local organizations and individuals in rural areas to advocate for their rights and development.

These objectives aim to use the legal system as a tool for positive change and development in rural communities.

RATIONAL OF THE STUDY

Rational of studying law for rural development is important for several reasons:

Legal Framework: Understanding the legal framework is essential for creating policies and regulations that support rural development. Laws can address land rights, agricultural practices, environmental conservation, and more.

Access to Justice: Rural communities often face unique legal challenges. Studying law can empower individuals in rural areas to access justice, protect their rights, and address issues such as land disputes, labor rights, and social justice.

i) Advocacy: Legal knowledge equips individuals and organizations to advocate for rural development initiatives, lobby for policy changes, and address social injustices that can hinder rural progress.

ii) Land Rights: Land is a crucial asset in rural areas. Knowledge of property and land laws is essential for protecting the rights of rural landowners, preventing land grabs, and promoting equitable access to land resources.

iii) Environmental Protection: Rural development must consider sustainable environmental practices. Legal expertise is needed to enforce environmental regulations, protect natural resources, and promote eco-friendly rural development.

iv) Economic Development: Legal knowledge can help foster economic growth in rural areas by facilitating business transactions, addressing regulatory barriers, and supporting entrepreneurship.

v) Social Justice: Rural areas often face issues related to social equity, such as access to education, healthcare, and social services. Legal tools are vital for addressing these disparities. In summary, studying law for rural development is essential for creating a legal framework that promotes social and economic progress in rural communities, ensures justice, and protects the rights and resources of those living in these areas.

REVIEW OF LITERATURE

A review of the literature on law for rural development would involve examining existing research and scholarly works that address the legal aspects of rural development. Such a review would typically cover a range of topics, including land rights, agricultural law, environmental regulations, and social justice issues. Here's a brief overview of what such a review might include:

Land Tenure and Property Rights: Analyze studies and legal frameworks related to land tenure systems, land reform, and property rights in rural areas. Discuss the impact of secure land tenure on agricultural productivity and rural development.

i) Agricultural Law and Policy: Examine the legal and policy frameworks governing agriculture in rural areas. Discuss the role of agricultural subsidies, regulations, and trade agreements in shaping rural development.

ii) Environmental Regulations: Explore how environmental laws and regulations affect rural communities, particularly in terms of land use, natural resource management, and conservation efforts.

iii) Access to Justice: Discuss the availability and accessibility of legal services in rural areas. Analyze the role of legal aid programs and the justice system in addressing rural development challenges.

iv) Social Justice and Rural Development: Investigate the legal aspects of social justice issues in rural development, such as gender equality, indigenous rights, and equitable access to resources and services. Case Studies and Best Practices: Highlight specific case studies, successful legal interventions, and best practices that have positively impacted rural development in various regions. Challenges and Gaps: Identify the challenges and gaps in the legal framework for rural development, such as land conflicts, limited legal awareness, and enforcement issues.

v) Future Directions: Suggest areas for further research and potential legal reforms that could enhance rural development outcomes. Literature review should synthesize and critically analyze existing literature in these areas, providing insights into the legal dimensions of rural development and the opportunities for legal reform to support rural communities' progress.

CHAPTER TWO

# LAW FOR SOCIAL DEVELOPMENT OF RURAL PEOPLE

# Prohibition of Sati Act 1829, Sati Abolition Act

**Sati Abolition Act of 1829, also known as the Bengal Sati Regulation, was landmark legislation passed by the British East India Company that banned the practice of Sati or the immolation of widows on their funeral pyre of husbands. The act was a significant step towards the reform of Indian society and marked the beginning of a series of social reforms initiated by the British colonial administration in India.**

*The Bengal Sati Regulation, 1829*

*Bengal Regulation 17 of 1829*

A Regulation for declaring the practice of sati or of burning or burying alive the widows of Hindus illegal and punishable by the Criminal Courts.

**1. Preamble.** - The practice of sati or of burning or burying alive the widows of Hindus is revolting to the feelings of human nature ; it is nowhere enjoined by the religion of the Hindus as an imperative duty ; on the contrary, a life of purity and retirement on the part of the widow is more especially and preferably inculcated, and by a vast majority of that people throughout India the practice is not kept up nor observed ; in some extensive districts it does not exist; in those in which it has been more frequent it is notorious that in many instances acts of atrocity have been perpetrated which have been shocking to the Hindus themselves and in their eyes unlawful and wicked.

The measures hitherto adopted to discourage and prevent such acts have failed of success, and the Governor General in Council is deeply impressed with the conviction that the abuses in question cannot be effectually put an end to without abolishing the practice altogether.

**2. Sati declared illegal and punishable.** - The practice of sati or burning or burying alive the widows of Hindus is hereby declared illegal and punishable by Criminal Courts.

**3. First.** - Zamindars etc., responsible for immediate communication to police of intended sacrifice. - All zamindars, talukdars or other proprietors of land, whether malguzari or lakhiraj, all sadar farmers and under renters of land of every description, all dependant talukdars, all naibs and other local agents, all officers employed in the collection of the revenue and rents of lands on the part of Government or the Court of Wards and all Mandals or other headmen of villages, are hereby declared especially accountable for the immediate communication to the officers of the nearest police-station of any intended sacrifice of the nature described in the foregoing section; and any zamindar or other description of persons above noticed, to whom such responsibility is declared to attach, who may be convicted of wilfully neglecting or delaying to furnish the information above required, shall be liable to be fined by the Magistrate or Joint Magistrate in any sum not exceeding two hundred rupees, and in default of payment to be confined for any period of imprisonment not exceeding six months.

**Second.** - Police how to act on receiving intelligence of intended sacrifice. - Immediately on receiving intelligence that the sacrifice declared illegal by this Regulation is likely to occur, the police daroga shall either report in person to the spot, or depute his muharrir or jamadar accompanied by one or more barkandazes and it shall be the duty of the police-officers to announce to the persons assembled for the performance of the ceremony that it is illegal, and to endeavour to prevail on them to disperse, explaining to them that, in the event of their persisting in it, they will involve themselves in a crime and become subject to punishment by the Criminal Courts.

Should the parties assembled proceed in defiance of these remonstrances to carry the ceremony into effect, it shall be the duty of the police-officers to use all lawful means in their power to prevent the sacrifice from raking place, and to apprehend the principal persons aiding and abetting in the performance of it; and in the event of the police-officers being unable to apprehend them they shall endeavour to ascertain their names and places of abode, and shall immediately communicate the whole of the particulars to the Magistrate or Joint Magistrate for his orders.

**Third.** - How to act when intelligence of sacrifice does not reach them until after it has taken place. - Should intelligence of a sacrifice declared illegal by this Regulation not reach the police-officers until after it shall have actually taken place, or should the sacrifice have been carried into effect before their arrival at the spot, they will nevertheless institute a full inquiry into the circumstances of the case, in like manner as on all other occasions of unnatural death, and report them for the information and orders of the Magistrate or Joint Magistrate to whom they may be subordinate.

**4-5.** Trial of persons concerned in the sacrifice; sentence or death by Court of Nizamat Adalat. - Repealed by Act 17 of 1862

# The Child Marriage Restraint Act, 1929

It is also known as the Sharda Act, was a significant legislative step taken in India to address the harmful practice of child marriage. Here are the key provisions of the Act:

**Short Title and Extent:**

The Act may be called the Child Marriage Restraint Act, 1929.

It extends to the whole of India (except the State of Jammu and Kashmir) and applies to all citizens of India, both within and beyond its borders.

The Act came into force on the $1^{st}$ day of April, 1930.

**Definitions:**

Child: Refers to a person who, if male, has not completed twenty-one years of age, and if female, has not completed eighteen years of age.

**Child Marriage:** Refers to a marriage in which either of the contracting parties is a child.

Contracting Party: Refers to either of the parties whose marriage is (or is about to be) solemnized.

**Minor**: Refers to a person of either sex who is under eighteen years of age.

**Punishments:**

Male Adult Below Twenty-One: If a male above eighteen years of age and below twenty-one contracts a child marriage, he shall be punishable with simple imprisonment (up to fifteen days), or with a fine (up to one thousand rupees), or both.

Male Adult Above Twenty-One: If a male above twenty-one years of age contracts a child marriage, he shall be punishable with simple imprisonment (up to three months) and shall also be liable to fine.

Solemnizing a Child Marriage: Anyone who performs, conducts, or directs a child marriage shall be punishable with simple imprisonment (up to three months) and liable to fine, unless they prove that they had reason to believe the marriage was not a child marriage.

Parent or Guardian Concerned in a Child Marriage: If a minor contracts a child marriage, any person having charge of the minor (whether as a parent, guardian, or in any other capacity) who promotes or permits the marriage shall be punishable with simple imprisonment (up to three months) and liable to fine. However, no woman shall be punishable with imprisonment.

**Objective:**

The Act aimed to eradicate the evil of child marriage, safeguarding the life and health of young girls who were unable to withstand the challenges of early married life and preventing premature deaths of minor mothers

# The Prohibition of Child Marriage Act, 2006 (PCMA)

It came into force in India on 1st November 2007. This crucial legislation aims to prevent child marriages and provide assistance to the victims of such marriages.

Here are some key provisions of the Act:

Definitions:

Child: Refers to a person who, if male, has not completed twenty-one years of age, and if female, has not completed eighteen years of age.

Child Marriage: Refers to a marriage in which either of the contracting parties is a child.

Contracting Party: Refers to either of the parties whose marriage is (or is about to be) solemnized.

Child Marriage Prohibition Officer: Includes the officer appointed under the Act to enforce its provisions.

1. Voidable Marriages:Child marriages are considered voidable at the option of the contracting party who is a child. This means that the marriage can be annulled if either party chooses to do so.

2. Maintenance and Residence: The Act provides for maintenance and residence to the female contracting party in a child marriage.

3. Custody and Maintenance of Children:The Act addresses the custody and maintenance of children born out of child marriages.

4.Legitimacy of Children: Children born from child marriages are considered legitimate.

5. Punishments: The Act prescribes punishments for various offenses related to child marriages, including marrying a child, solemnizing a child marriage, and promoting or permitting such marriages.

6. Injunctions and Void Marriages: Courts have the power to issue injunctions prohibiting child marriages. Child marriages conducted in contravention of injunction orders are considered void.

7. Enforcement:The Act designates Child Marriage Prohibition Officers to enforce its provisions.

8. Protection of Action Taken in Good Faith: Officers acting in good faith while enforcing the Act are protected from legal action

9. Rules and Repeal: The Act empowers the State Government to make rules. It also amends Act No. 25 of 1955 (the Child Marriage Restraint Act of 1929). The Act repeals the earlier legislation on child marriage. The PCMA plays a crucial role in safeguarding the rights and well-being of children, ensuring that they are not forced into early marriages. It reflects India's commitment to eradicating this harmful practice and promoting a safer and healthier future for its youth

# Prohibition of Child Marriage (Amendment) Bill 2021

The decision to raise the legal marriage age for women from 18 to 21 years old was approved by the Union Cabinet on December 15, 2021. Therefore, if a girl marries before the age of 21, it would be regarded as child marriage and will be penalized under the Prohibition of Child Marriage Act of 2006. As the legal marriage age for men in India is likewise 21, the basis for this modification is the implementation of the constitutional duty for gender equality.

# HINDU MARRIAGE ACT, 1955

## GENERAL INRODUCTION

Marriage has been considered as the greatest and the most important of all the social institutions. For the Hindus, it is considered as a means to lay the foundation for building up the family which is the basic unit of any society. Since marriage holds such a great significance in the society, it is necessary for the legislature to come up with the proper legislation which deals with the governance of marriages in the country. Therefore, the Hindu Marriage Act, 1955 was enacted to amend and codify the laws relating to Hindu marriages. It has reformed Hindu law of marriage. It has not only codified the Hindu marriage law but also introduced certain important changes in many respects. The Hindu Marriage Act, 1955 came into force on 18th May 1955 with the objective to secure and protect the right to marriage of the Hindu men and women. In India the right to marriage has not been explicitly provided anywhere. Although its essence can be found in Article 21 of Indian Constitution.

The Hindu Marriage Act, 1955 regulates the institution of marriage of Hindus in Indian society. It provides meaning to marriage, cohabiting rights of both the bride and groom and a safety to their family and children.

## KEY FEATURES OF THE HINDU MARRIAGE ACT, 1955

1. Applicability of the act and who all are Hindus according to HMA, 1955: This law extends to the whole of India except the state of Jammu and Kashmir. It applies to all forms of Hinduism. Under section 2(1) of the act any person would be considered as 'Hindu' for the purpose of law, if he is:

A person who is Hindu by religion in any of its forms and developments;
A person professing the Hindu, Buddhist, Jain or Sikh religion.
A person who is not a Christian, Muslim, Jew or Parsi by religion will be governed by Hindu Law unless it is proved that such person will not be governed by Hindu Law.

2. Essential Conditions for valid marriage: section 5 of HMA, 1955 specifies certain conditions for the valid Hindu marriage, they are as follows:-

Monogamy – monogamy means that a Hindu is permitted to have only one spouse at a time. It is clearly stated in section 5 (i) of the act that neither party has a spouse living at the time of the marriage and in case one contravene such conditions then it will render that marriage void.
Soundness of spouses – section 5 (ii) of the act provides that the parties to the marriage should be of sound mind and are not suffering from any kind of mental disorder so as to be unsuitable for giving a valid consent.
Minimum age for marriage – section 5 (iii) fixed the minimum age for the men and women. The women and men should complete the age of 18 years and 21 years.
Beyond prohibited degree – section 5 (iv) provides that the persons who are within the prohibited degree of relationship cannot marry with each other. Unless the custom or the usage of parties permits.
Beyond sapinda relationship – section 5 (v) provides that the parties to the marriage must not be sapindas of each other unless their customs or usages permits the marriage.
Ceremonies and registration of marriage: section 7 and 8 of the HMA, 1955 deals with the ceremonies and the registration of the Hindu marriage. Section 7 laid down that the Hindu marriage can be solemnized by following the rites and ceremonies of either party to the marriage. But this section nowhere makes any ceremony or rites compulsory to perform to determine the validity of the marriage. In the case of Chandrabhagbai Ganpati v S.N. Kanwar[1] It was held that the marriage was legal notwithstanding the fact that the marriage ceremonies did not include saptapadi.
Section 8 lays down the provisions regarding registration of marriage but it did not make registration mandatory. Non registration of marriage will not make the marriage invalid. In the case of Kamal Kant Panduranga v. Susheeela Panduranga Chibde, Bombay High Court held that any provisions in the rules invalidating a marriage because of omission to enter the same in the marriage register would be impugned to section 8 (5) of the act.

4. Matrimonial Remedies: section 9 to 13 of the Hindu Marriage Act, 1955 discusses the matrimonial remedies available to both the parties to the marriage. They are as follows:

A. Restitution of Conjugal rights (section 9) – the decree of restitution of conjugal right issued under order XXI rule 32 of Code of Civil Procedure. It is the right available to both the parties to the marriage when one spouse leaves the conjugal life or the marital society of another without any reasonable excuse.

Its Essentials:-

The other spouse has to be withdrawn from the society of another spouse.
There should be no reasonable excuse of such withdrawal.
The court satisfaction as to the truth of the statement made in the petition.
No legal grounds exist for refusing the petition.
B. Judicial Separation (section 10) – the decree of judicial separation permits the parties to live apart from each other for some period of time but it does not put an end to the marriage, the legal relationship between the couple exists and they cannot remarry. The purpose is to enable the spouses to reconsider their relationship and try to resolve the issues in their marriage. The grounds to apply for judicial separation are the same as for divorce (section 13).

In the case of Narasimha Reddy v Basamma[2], it was held that when parties are not judicially separate neither spouse can contract another marriage. A marriage after a separation decree and before divorce was held to amount bigamy.

C. Nullity of Marriage [Void and Voidable Marriages]:

Void Marriage –Void marriages have no legal status. It is void ab initio and may be declared nullity at the instance of either party. Section 11 of HMA, 1955 specifies when a marriage will be declared as void. If a marriage is solemnized in contravention of following conditions than it is void:-

Either party has a spouse living at the time of the marriage.
Parties are within the degrees of prohibited relationship.
Parties are sapindas to each other.
Voidable Marriages – Section 12 of HMA, 1955 defines when a marriage is considered as voidable marriage. When:

If one of the spouses is impotent.
If one of the spouses is mentally unfit.
If consent was not free. It was taken due to fraud or misrepresentation.
If the woman is pregnant already at the time of marriage with someone else's child.
In the case of Mahendra v Sushila Bai[3]Sushila Bai delivered a child within 171 days of her marriage. Court held that this was not with the relationship of Mahendra but she had a relationship before the marriage itself. In this case this marriage is considered as voidable marriage.

D. Divorce (section 13): Divorce is the permanent dissolution of marriage. Section 13 –B gives provision regarding divorce by mutual consent of both the spouses. Under section 13(1) of HMA, 1955, there are grounds on which both the spouses can seek divorce and in addition to the previous grounds wife has additional grounds on which she can file a divorce petition which are specified under section 13(2). So the grounds are as follows:

Adultery [section 13 (1) (i)] – adultery is having voluntary sexual intercourse between a married person with any person other than his or her wife or husband. In the case of Kamalesh Kumari v Balbir Singh Bedi[4], husband and wife have not met for 11 months and 20 days and yet wife got pregnant. So there was circumstantial proof that there is adultery.
Cruelty [section 13 (ia)] – In the case of Russel v Russel, 1897, Court has defined what is cruelty, "Conduct of such a character as to have caused danger to life, limb or health bodily or mental or as to give rise to a reasonable apprehension of such danger".

Desertion [section 13 (ib)] – In the case of Bipin Chandra Jai Singh Bai Shah v Prabhavati[5], the Court gives essential conditions for desertion – Intention on part of the spouse who is leaving to live separately.[6]
Intention to bring cohabitation to an end permanently.
Without reasonable cause.
Without consent or wish of the deserted spouse.
Conversion [section 13 (1) (ii)] – it means any person who ceases to be Hindu by conversion to another religion. In the case of Sarla Mudgal v Union of India[7], in this case there was a Hindu married man. Still he married again by converting to Islam. The court held the second marriage is void and punishable for bigamy.
Insanity [section 13 (1) (iii)] – if either spouse is suffering from unsoundness of mind then it would be a valid ground for divorce.
Leprosy is now removed as a ground for divorce by personal law (amendment) act, 2019.
Venereal Disease [section 13 (1) (v)] – a disease that can be transmitted through sexual contact is venereal disease. If either party to the marriage is suffering from venereal then this can be considered as a ground for divorce.
Renounced the world [section 13 (1) (vi)] – if either party has renounced the world and entered into any religious order in that case the aggrieved party can apply for divorce.
Presumption of death [section 13 (1) (vii)] – when either party to the divorce has not been heard for seven consecutive years and the people who should know whether that party is alive or not are not aware about the same. In that case the party left behind can apply divorce on this ground.
Non resumption of cohabitation after the decree of judicial separation and decree of restitution of conjugal rights is passed [ section 13 (1-A) (i) and (ii)] – if the parties do not intend to resume their marital life despite court decree then it is desirable to treat that marriage as beyond repair. So the decree of divorce is passed on these grounds also.
Additional grounds available to wife under section 13 (2) of HMA, 1955 are as follows:

Bigamy – Bigamy is the offence of marrying again while already being married. So Hindu wife can apply for divorce if her husband is guilty of bigamy.

Sexual offences – if the husband has, since the solemnization of the marriage been guilty of rape, sodomy (anal sex) and bestiality (unnatural sex) then wife can apply for divorce.

Non resumption of marriage after the decree of maintenance – the third important ground available for a wife is no resumption of marriage after a decree of maintenance is given for one year and after one year of such separation they are not cohabiting. In that case the wife can apply for divorce. But it is necessary that there is no cohabitation between husband and wife. In the case of B. Nausea v B Rakaia, wife took a decree for separation. However later lived with her husband. Courts held that such living brings end to maintenance.

Repudiation of marriage – section 13 (2) (iv) of the Hindu Marriage Act, 1955 discusses repudiation of marriage on the option of puberty of the girl. She can apply for divorce between the ages of 15 to 18 and once she attains the age of 18 years she cannot apply for divorce.

## CONCLUSION

The Hindu Marriage Act, 1955 has come up with so many vital and diverse changes in the Hindu marriage and divorce that it changes the whole concept of it. Now the Hindu marriage is not only considered as a sacred one but now it also has contains some of the features of contract for example- the party to the marriage has to be major, the consent of both of them is essential. It has reformed the Hindu law of marriage to the greater extent.

[1] 2008 MLR 21 (Bom.)

[2] AIR 1976 AP 77

[3] 1965 AIR 364

[4] AIR 1973 P H 152

[5] 1956 SCR 838

[7] AIR 1995 SC 1531

CHAPTER THREE

# LAW FOR JUDICIAL / LEGAL DEVELOPMENT OF RURAL PEOPLE

# GRAM NYAYALAYAS ACT, 2008

This act provide for the establishment of Gram Nyayalayas at the grass roots level for the purposes of providing access to justice to the citizens at their doorsteps and to ensure that opportunities for securing justice are not denied to any citizen by reason of social, economic or other disabilities and for matters connected therewith or incidental thereto.

It establishes Gram Nyayalayas or village courts for speedy and easy access to justice system in the rural areas of India. The Act came into force from 2 October 2009. However, the Act has not been enforced properly, with only 208 functional Gram Nyayalayas in the country (as of 3 September 2019) against a target of 5000 such courts. The major reasons behind the non-enforcement includes financial constraints, reluctance of lawyers, police and other government officials.

The Gram Nyayalayas are presided over by a Nyayadhikari, who will have the same power, enjoy same salary and benefits of a Judicial Magistrate of First Class who are to be appointed by the State Government in consultation with the respective High Court. Civil suits are proceeded on a day-to-day basis, with limited adjournments and are to be disposed of within a period of six months from the date of institution of the suit. Gram Nyayalayas has been given power to accept certain evidences which would otherwise not be acceptable under Indian Evidence Act. Appeals in criminal matter can be made to the Sessions Court in the respective jurisdiction and in civil matters to the District Court within a period of one month from the date of judgment.

# THE LEGAL SERVICES AUTHORITIES ACT, 1987

## Introduction

The Legal Services Authorities Act, 1987, was enacted by the Central Government of India pursuant to Article 39-A of the Constitution of India and the recommendations of its committees. It came into effect on 9th November 1995, following the Amendment Act of 1994, which introduced several amendments to the main Act. According to this Act, the economically weak, the backward, and the disabled are eligible to receive legal aid. In 1971, Justice P. N. Bhagawati introduced the legal aid scheme, which was overseen by the Legal Aid Committee. On 5th December 1995, the National Legal Services Authority was established by Justice R. N. Mishra, which was an important contribution to the implementation of the Act.

Anyone who qualifies for legal aid under Section 12 of the Act, may obtain legal assistance under the Act. The legal aid is to be provided by the State, District, and Taluk Legal Service Authorities/Commissions formed throughout the country in order to bring about a re-dedication to ensure equality of opportunity and fairness to all individuals. Through its various forms of legal assistance, it promotes equal opportunity and justice for all citizens.

The Act envisions that no one will be denied access to justice because of disability or economic reasons, and aims to educate the public about the law, offer free legal aid, and establish Lok Adalats.

The Act provides many types of legal services to the general public:

### *Free legal awareness*

This Act is primarily intended for the public to make them aware of laws and schemes issued by public authorities. The Legal Service Authority teaches some portions of the rules of law to the individuals. Legal camps and legal aid centres are organized by authorities so that the general public can seek advice from the legal aid centres located near their homes or places of work. The legal guides and centres can help address the grievances of ordinary people as well.

## *Free legal aid counsel*

A person who wants to defend or file a case in a court of law but does not have the means to hire an advocate can seek the assistance of a free legal aid attorney. The Act states that free legal aid counsel is available, and the Council is responsible for assisting needy individuals to obtain justice. By adopting and establishing this philosophy, the Indian Courts should be freed from the burden of adjudicating the cases.

A Lok Adalat was held for the first time in Gujarat on 14$^{th}$ March 1982 and succeeded in resolving many disputes pertaining to labour disputes, family disputes, and bank recoveries. Lok Adalats are the primary method by which the legal services authorities decide disputes. Lok Adalat was, thus, seen as an Alternative Dispute Redressal (ADR) mechanism that was reliable, efficient, and friendly in resolving disputes. Lok Adalats can be constituted by the legal services authorities at such spans and locations to exercise the authority of their jurisdiction in such areas as they think fit.

## *Objectives of Legal Services Authority Act:*

Under Article 39A of the Constitution of India, free legal aid and equal justice are provided to all citizens by appropriate legislation, schemes or other means to ensure that no citizen is denied access to justice on the basis of economic disadvantage or in any other way. The Legal Services Authorities Act, 1987 was enacted as a consequence of this constitutional provision with the primary objective of providing free and competent legal services to the weaker sections of society in the country.

## *Structural Organization under Legal Services Authority Act:*

As a result of the Legal Services Act, a National Legal Services Authority (NALSA) was established as the apex body for regulating the legal aid provisions. State Legal Services Authority (SALSA) handles the implementation of NALSA's powers at the state level, which delegates further to a number of organizations. NALSA is considered to be an alliance between the State, Social Action Groups, individuals, and non-profit organizations that have their presence from the grassroots level to the state level.

### *NALSA*

CHAPTER FOUR

# LAW FOR EDUCATIONAL DEVELOPMENT OF RURAL PEOPLE

Education plays an integral role in the overall progress of rural areas. First of all, education introduces one to new and innovative ideas to improve his/her social condition. Educating the rural population at an early age ensures that there is no discrimination between the urban and rural populations. Therefore, they are open to countless employment opportunities from multiple sectors and industries.

# THE INDIRA GANDHI NATIONAL OPEN UNIVERSITY ACT, 1985

The Indira Gandhi National Open University (IGNOU), established by an Act of Parliament in 1985, has continuously striven to build an inclusive knowledge society through inclusive education. It has tried to increase the Gross Enrollment Ratio (GER) by offering high-quality teaching through the Open and Distance Learning (ODL) mode.

The University began by offering two academic programmes in 1987, i.e., Diploma in Management and Diploma in Distance Education, with a strength of 4,528 students.

Today, it serves the educational aspirations of over 3 million students in India and other countries through 21 Schools of Studies and a network of 67 Regional Centres, around 2,000 Learner Support Centres and 20 overseas institutions. The University offers about 200 certificate, diploma, degree and doctoral programmes, with a strength of nearly 250 faculty members and 230 academic staff at the headquarters and regional centres and over 35,000 academic counsellors from conventional institutions of higher learning, professional organisations, and industry among others.

The mandate of the University is to:

1. Provide access to higher education to all segments of the society;

2. Offer high-quality, innovative and need-based programmes at different levels, to all those who require them;

3. Reach out to the disadvantaged by offering programmes in all parts of the country at affordable costs; and

4. Promote, coordinate and regulate the standards of education offered through open and distance learning in the country.

5. To achieve the twin objectives of widening access for all sections of society and providing continual professional development and training to all sectors of the economy, the University uses a variety of media and latest technology in imparting education. This is reflected in the formulated vision of IGNOU, keeping its objectives in focus, which reads:

The Indira Gandhi National Open University, the National Resource Centre for Open and Distance Learning, with international recognition and presence, shall provide seamless access to sustainable and learner-centric quality education, skill upgradation and training to all by using innovative technologies and methodologies and ensuring convergence of existing systems for large-scale human resource development, required for promoting integrated national development and global understanding.

The University has made a significant mark in the areas of higher education, community education and continual professional development. The University has been networking with reputed public institutions and private enterprises for enhancing the educational opportunities being offered by it. As a world leader in distance education, it has been conferred with awards of excellence by the Commonwealth of Learning (COL), Canada.

The University is committed to quality in teaching, research, training and extension activities, and acts as a national resource centre for expertise and infrastructure in the ODL system. The University has established the National Centre for Disability Studies and National Centre for Innovation in Distance Education, to focus on specific learner groups and enrich the distance learning system.

With the launch of EduSat (a satellite dedicated only to education) on 20th September, 2004, and the establishment of the Inter-University Consortium, the University has ushered in a new era of technology-enabled education in the country. All the regional centres and high enrollment Learners Support have been provided with active two-way video-conferencing network connectivity, which has made it possible to transact interactive digital content.

Emphasis is now being laid on developing interactive multimedia and online learning, and adding value to the traditional distance education delivery mode with modern technology-enabled education within the framework of integrated distance and online learning.

Over the years, IGNOU has lived up to the country's expectations of providing education to the marginalised sections of society. Free of cost education is being provided to all jail inmates across the country. A large number of SC/ST students have been admitted to various programmes of the University, also efforts have been made to reach onto persons working in the Armed and Security Forces of the Country. Thus this act of parliament is playing a very vital role in the higher education system to the people of rural area also.

# RIGHT TO EDUCATION (RTE) ACT 2009

The Parliament enacted the Right to Education Act 2009 (RTE Act) intending to regulate the degradation of the standard of the education system and to uplift the education imparting procedure by implementing specific provisions that required certain reformations to live up to the spirit of catering a quality and equitable education irrespective of caste, creed, gender economic and social background. The Act was enacted on 4th August 2009 and came into force on 1st April 2010. The principal features of the Act are as follows:

1. The Act clearly mentions that education is the Fundamental Right of every child.
2. Private schools must keep 25% of seats reserved for children belonging to the backward classes in terms of social background.
3. The Act also assures educational rights for dropout students.
4. Unrecognized schools are barred from interviewing a child or a parent for admission.
5. Schools are barred from charging any capitation fees at any step while providing admission to a child.
6. Children pursuing elementary education shall not be expelled, held back, or pressured to pass a board examination.
7. The Act mandates that every government and aided schools create a School Management Committee composed of 75% of members as parents or guardians.
8. The Act prohibited physical punishment, mental harassment and private tuition by the teachers.
9. The Act states the provisions for a child's admission to an appropriate class based on his/her age in the event that child has never been admitted to any school. To help keep up the child with other students, provisions relating to special training have also been mentioned in the Act.

The RTE Act 2009 acted as a catalyst in accelerating the spirit of imparting free and compulsory elementary education to children between the age group of 6 to 14 years. Subsequent to the inception of the Act, a drastic change came about in the standard of education both in access and enrolment levels; literacy rates of the states also elevated at large. However, lately, due to a lack of an appropriate regulatory framework, the practical application and compliance with the provisions of the Act are facing repeated failure

CHAPTER FIVE

# LAW FOR MEDICAL / HEALTHCARE DEVELOPMENT OF RURAL PEOPLE

Healthcare is an important part of rural development in India. The rural population is often susceptible to diseases that can be avoided with proper healthcare measures. Besides, this contributes directly to their productivity.

As a result, they will be able to participate in healthy competitions in the market. Proper healthcare systems also reduce the mortality rate, thus ensuring a healthy and meaningful life.

In addition, access to clean drinkable water and sanitation is a must for the development of rural areas. In this way, rural residents will be able to benefit from equal income opportunities and sustainable healthcare services.

That right to good health is the fundamental right to every citizen of India under Article 21 of Constitution of India.

The Cigarettes and Other tobacco products (prohibition of advertisement and regulation of trade and commerce, production, supply and distribution) act, 2003 no. 34 of 2003

# EPIDEMIC DISEASES ACT 1897

The epidemic disease act 1897 is colonial Era law enacted to tackles the bubonic plague in Mumbai than Bombay during British rule in India. The act provides Special Powers to both Central and state government to implement measures necessary to control the spread of dangerous epidemic diseases.

The act allows state government to take a special measure and prescribe regulation to prevent the outbreak or spread of an epidemic. The central government can also take measure especially conserving the inspection and detection of ships or vessels. Violation of regulation under this act is punishable under section 188 of the Indian Penal Code. The individual acting in good faith under the set are protected from legal proceedings. In response to the covid-19 pandemic the Act was amended to include provisions for punishing those who attack Health Care workers the amendment allows for up to 7 years of imprisonment for such offences.

CHAPTER SIX

# LAW FOR POLITICAL DEVELOPMENT OF RURAL PEOPLE

# 73RD CONSTITUTIONAL AMENDMENT ACT OF 1992

Significance of the Act

- The Act added Part IX to the Constitution, "The Panchayats" and also added the Eleventh Schedule which consists of the 29 functional items of the panchayats.
- Part IX of the Constitution contains Article 243 to Article 243 O.
- The Amendment Act provides shape to Article 40 of the Constitution, (directive principles of state policy), which directs the state to organise the village panchayats and provide them powers and authority so that they can function as self-government.
- With the Act, Panchayati Raj systems come under the purview of the justiciable part of the Constitution and mandates states to adopt the system. Further, the election process in the Panchayati Raj institutions will be held independent of the state government's will.
- The Act has two parts: compulsory and voluntary. Compulsory provisions must be added to state laws, which includes the creation of the new Panchayati Raj systems. Voluntary provisions, on the other hand, is the discretion of the state government.
- The Act is a very significant step in creating democratic institutions at the grassroots level in the country. The Act has transformed the representative democracy into participatory democracy.

**Salient Features of the Act**

1. Gram Sabha: Gram Sabha is the primary body of the Panchayati Raj system. It is a village assembly consisting of all the registered voters within the area of the panchayat. It will exercise powers and perform such functions as determined by the state legislature. Candidates can refer to the functions of gram panchayat and gram panchayat work, on the government official website – https://grammanchitra.gov.in/.

2. Three-tier system: The Act provides for the establishment of the three-tier system of Panchayati Raj in the states (village, intermediate and district level). States with a population of less than 20 lakhs may not constitute the intermediate level.
3. Election of members and chairperson: The members to all the levels of the Panchayati Raj are elected directly and the chairpersons to the intermediate and the district level are elected indirectly from the elected members and at the village level the Chairperson is elected as determined by the state government.
4. The Chairperson of a Panchayat and other members of a Panchayat, whether or not elected directly from territorial constituencies in the Panchayat area, have the right to vote in Panchayat meetings.
5. Reservation of seats:

- For SC and ST: Reservation to be provided at all the three tiers in accordance with their population percentage.
- For women: Not less than one-third of the total number of seats to be reserved for women, further not less than one-third of the total number of offices for chairperson at all levels of the panchayat to be reserved for women.
- The state legislatures are also given the provision to decide on the reservation of seats in any level of panchayat or office of chairperson in favour of backward classes.

6. Duration of Panchayat: The Act provides for a five-year term of office to all the levels of the panchayat. However, the panchayat can be dissolved before the completion of its term. But fresh elections to constitute the new panchayat shall be completed –

- before the expiry of its five-year duration.
- in case of dissolution, before the expiry of a period of six months from the date of its dissolution.

7. Disqualification: A person shall be disqualified for being chosen as or for being a member of panchayat if he is so disqualified –

- Under any law for the time being in force for the purpose of elections to the legislature of the state concerned.
- Under any law made by the state legislature. However, no person shall be disqualified on the ground that he is less than 25 years of age if he has attained the age of 21 years.
- Further, all questions relating to disqualification shall be referred to an authority determined by the state legislatures

8. Election commission:

- The commission is responsible for superintendence, direction and control of the preparation of electoral rolls and conducting elections for the panchayat.
- The state legislature may make provisions with respect to all matters relating to elections to the panchayats.
- Powers and Functions: The state legislature may endow the Panchayats with such powers and authority as may be necessary to enable them to function as institutions of self-government. Such a scheme may contain provisions related to Gram Panchayat work with respect to:
  a) the preparation of plans for economic development and social justice.
  b) the implementation of schemes for economic development and social justice as may be entrusted to them, including those in relation to the 29 matters listed in the Eleventh Schedule.

9. Finances: The state legislature may –

- Authorize a panchayat to levy, collect and appropriate taxes, duties, tolls and fees.
- Assign to a panchayat taxes, duties, tolls and fees levied and collected by the state government.
- Provide for making grants-in-aid to the panchayats from the consolidated fund of the state.
- Provide for the constitution of funds for crediting all money of the panchayats.

**Finance Commission**: The state finance commission reviews the financial position of the panchayats and provides recommendations for the necessary steps to be taken to supplement resources to the panchayat.

Audit of Accounts: State legislature may make provisions for the maintenance and audit of panchayat accounts.

Application to Union Territories: The President may direct the provisions of the Act to be applied on any union territory subject to exceptions and modifications he specifies.

Exempted states and areas: The Act does not apply to the states of Nagaland, Meghalaya and Mizoram and certain other areas. These areas include,

a) The scheduled areas and the tribal areas in the states

b) The hill area of Manipur for which a district council exists

c) Darjeeling district of West Bengal for which Darjeeling Gorkha Hill Council exists.

However, Parliament can extend this part to these areas subject to the exception and modification it specifies. Thus, the PESA Act was enacted.

1. of existing law: All the state laws relating to panchayats shall continue to be in force until the expiry of one year from the commencement of this Act. In other words, the states have to adopt the new Panchayati raj system based on this Act within the maximum period of one year from 24 April 1993, which was the date of the commencement of this Act. However, all the Panchayats existing immediately before the commencement of the Act shall continue till the expiry of their term, unless dissolved by the state legislature sooner.
2. to interference by courts: The Act bars the courts from interfering in the electoral matters of panchayats. It declares that the validity of any law relating to the delimitation of constituencies or the allotment of

seats to such constituencies cannot be questioned in any court. It further lays down that no election to any panchayat is to be questioned except by an election petition presented to such authority and in such manner as provided by the state legislature

CHAPTER SEVEN

# LAW FOR ECONOMIC DEVELOPMENT OF RURAL PEOPLE

# MAHATMA GANDHI NATIONAL RURAL EMPLOYMENT GUARANTEE ACT, 2005 NO. 42 OF 2005, (MGNREGA)

## *History:*

In 1991, the P.V Narashima Rao government proposed a pilot scheme for generating employment in rural areas with the following goals:

- Employment Generation for agricultural labour during the lean season.
- Infrastructure Development
- Enhanced Food Security

This scheme was called the Employment Assurance Scheme which later evolved into the MGNREGA after the merger with the Food for Work Programme in the early 2000s.

## *Objectives of MGNREGA:*

The Mahatma Gandhi National Rural Employment Guarantee Act (MGNREGA) has the following objectives:

- Provide 100 days of guaranteed wage employment to rural unskilled labour
- Increase economic security
- Decrease migration of labour from rural to urban areas

MGNREGA differentiates itself from earlier welfare schemes by taking a grassroots-driven approach to employment generation. The programs under the act are demand-driven and provide legal provisions for appeal in the case, work is not provided or payments are delayed. The scheme is funded by the central government which bears the full cost of unskilled labour and 75% of the cost of material for works undertaken under this law. The central and state governments audit the works undertaken under this act through annual reports prepared by CEGC (Central Employment Guarantee Council) and the SEGC (State Employment Guarantee Councils). These reports have to be presented by the incumbent government in the legislature.

A few salient features of the scheme are:

- It gives a significant amount of control to the Gram Panchayats for managing public works, strengthening Panchayati Raj Institutions. Gram Sabhas are free to accept or reject recommendations from Intermediate and District Panchayats.
- It incorporates accountability in its operational guidelines and ensures compliance and transparency at all levels.

Ever since the scheme was implemented, the number of jobs has increased by 240% in the past 10 years. The scheme has been successful in enhancing economic empowerment in rural India and helping overcome the exploitation of labour. The scheme has also diminished wage volatility and the gender pay gap in labour. This can be substantiated the by the following data available at the official site of MGNREGA:

1. 14.88 crores MGNREGA job cards have been issued (Active Job Cards – 9.3 crores)
2. 28.83 crores workers who gained employed under MGNREGA (2020-21) out of which active workers are 14.49 crores.

Role of Gram Sabha in MGNREGS **of Gram**

It lists down the works priority-wise w.r.t the potential of the local area

It monitors the work executed within the Gram Panchayat

It acts as the primary forum for the social audits

It also works as a platform to resolve all workers' queries related to any MGNREGA work

Role of Gram Panchayat in MGNREGA

It is authorized with the role to receive the job applications

After receiving the applications, it is responsible to verify them

All households are registered by the Gram Panchayat

The MGNREGS job cards are issued by the Gram Panchayat

It is responsible to allot work within 15 days from the application submission

It prepares an annual report that covers the achievement of the scheme

It holds Rozgar Diwas at every ward once a month

# THE HINDU SUCCESSION AMENDMENT ACT 2005

Son and a daughter have equal rights in the property after the death of the father. Amendment in Hindu succession act increased the women empowerment in India and now every daughter has right in the ancestral property of her father. Thus this act empowers women economically by having rights in the property.

CHAPTER EIGHT

# LAW FOR INFRASTRUCTURE DEVELOPMENT OF RURAL PEOPLE

**Infrastructure** – The infrastructural condition of a rural area has a direct link with its scale of development. Primarily, infrastructure consists of pucca roads, a consistent supply of electricity, and availability of transport. With these factors, governing bodies have been able to reduce connectivity issues related to these areas. As a result, there has been an increase in the efficiency of the supply of agricultural output to mainland markets all over India. Therefore the opportunity of income increases among the rural residents.

# THE STAGE-CARRIAGES ACT, 1861

This act is related to the rural people in this way that it describe which animal is to be used for carriage and which not and also describe about weight to be loaded by them.

The stage Carriers act 1861 is historical piece of legislation in India that was enacted to regulate and license stage carriage. The act define stage Carriers as any careers drawn by one or more horses used for conveying passengers for hire it mandates that all stage carriages must by magistrate or the Commissioner of police the license must include details such as number of passengers the weight of luggage and number of horses used to draw the carriage the act prescribes penalty for various offences such as operating an unlicensed carriage overloading or ill treating animals. License can be revert if the careers is found to be un-serviceable or unsafe

# THE ROAD TRANSPORT CORPORATIONS ACT, 1950

The Road Transport Corporation Act 1950 was enacted to facilitate the establishment and regulation of road transport corporations by State government in India. It allows state government to setup Road Transport Corporation to provide efficient adequate economical and coordinated Road Transport services. These corporations are incorporated entities managed by board of directors which includes a Chairman and other members appointed by the state government. The corporation have the power to operate Road Transport services acquire property and undertaken activity necessary for their operation and maintenance. The corporation has power to operate road transport service required property and undertake activities necessary for their operation and maintenance. The act outlines the financial management of Corporation including the creation of fund forming powers and maintenance of road and audits. It provide for formulation of rules and regulation for the operation of the corporations and prescribes penalty for non compliance.

# THE NATIONAL HIGHWAYS ACT, 1956

Due to this law rural area is now well connected with other part of country. It also provide fair compensation to rural people if their land is acquired for the purpose of making road. The national highway Act 1956 is an important peace of legislation in India that provides for declaration of certain Highways as national highways and addresses related matters. The act allow the central government to declare any Highway as National Highway through a notification in the official gazette

It grants the central government the power to acquire land for construction maintenance and operation of national highways and management National Highways in the Union and are managed and developed by the central government rules and regulations. The act empowers the central government to make laws for implementation of its provision.

# THE CENTRAL ROAD AND INFRASTRUCTURE FUND ACT, 2000

As per provision of this law fund of the central government is obtained by state government which is utilized for development of road in rural area also.

The central Road and infrastructure fund act 2000 was enacted to established fund for development and maintenance of national highways state roads and rural roads in India. The act provide for creation of certain road and infrastructure fund which is finance by tax on petrol and diesel. The fund collected are used for development and maintenance of national highways, railways project, improvement of safety in railways state and central roads and other Infrastructure Projects. CRIF is administered by Ministry of Finance which over see the allocation and utilization of fund. The act include provision for apportionment of fund by a committee to ensure proper distribution and utilization

# THE CONTROL OF NATIONAL HIGHWAYS (LAND AND TRAFFIC) ACT, 2002

The control of national highways (land and traffic) Act 2002 is designed to regulate land use and traffic on national highway in India. The act provides for the control of land within the boundary of national highways including the right of way and the removal of unauthorized occupations. It establishes Highway administration to oversee the management and regulation of national highways, regulating traffic on national highway to ensure safety and smooth flow. It also prescribes penalty for various offences such as unauthorized construction, encroachments and violation of traffic regulations. The act establishes tribunals to adjudicate disputes and appeals related to enforcement of its provision

# THE CARRIAGE BY ROAD ACT, 2007

This law helps to provide smooth carriage of goods by road to the different area including rural area. Carriage by road act 2007 is significant piece of legislation in India that regulates the activity of common carriers. The act came to regulate common carriers, limit their liability, and declare the value of goods delivered to them. This helps determine their liability for any loss of damage to the goods due to negligence or criminal acts by the carrier or their agents. It applies to the entire country except for the state of Jammu and Kashmir. The common carriers must be registered to operate legally. The act limits the liability of common Carriers and requires them to declare the value of goods they transport. Carriers must issue a good received for the consignment they transport. There are specific provisions for the carrier of goods that are dangerous or hazardous to human life. The act is supplementary by the Carriage by road rules 2011 which provide details regulation for its implementation.

# THE LAND ACQUISITION ACT (The right to fair compensation and transparency in land acquisition rehabilitation and resettlement act 2013)

The land acquisition act in India has undergone significant changes over the year initially the land acquisition act 1894 the world the process of land acquisition for public purpose hybrid was replaced by the right to fair compensation and transparency in land acquisition rehabilitation and resettlement act 2013 (often referred to as the LARR or RFCTLARR Act)

Land owner and those affected by the land acquisition. It also provides provision for the rehabilitation and resettlement of those displaced by land acquisition. The act mandates transparent process of land acquisition including public hearing and social impact assessment. For private project the consent of at least 80% of the affected family is required and for public private partnership project the consent of at least 70% is needed.

CHAPTER NINE

# LAW FOR TECHNOLOGICAL DEVELOPMENT OF RURAL PEOPLE

The role of technology in rural development is indisputable. First of all, modern production techniques in various sectors can actively increase their rate of production, which allows for a remarkable rise in the scale of economic activities in rural areas. On the other hand, the technology significantly reduces irrigation and quality issues. Therefore, the presence of appropriate technological means such as pumps, tractors is the make-or-break factor of rural development.

# THE RIGHT TO INFORMATION ACT, 2005

Due to this law people of village area can ask any questions from any authority through email even due to technological development. The Right to Information act 2005 is a Landmark resignation in India that empower citizens to access information under the control of public authorities promoting transparency and accountability in the working of government buy providing citizen with the right to access information. It covers all public authorities including the central and the state governments and any organisation substantially financed by the government. Citizens can file and RTI request to obtain information Public Information Officer Pi o r designated in each public authority to handle these requests. It mandates that information must be provided within 30 days of the request in case involving the life or Liberty of a person the information must be provided within 48 hours. There are certain information which is exempt from disclosure such as information affecting national security personal privacy and trade secrets. If a request is denied citizen can appeal to higher authority including Central information commission or state information commissions.

# THE INFORMATION TECHNOLOGY ACT, 2008

The information technology act 2000 also known as IT Act 2000 or IT Act is a significant peace of legislation in India that provides a legal Framework for electronic governance by recognising electronic records and digital signatures equivalent to paper based documents as per legal recognition. The act defines various Cyber crimes and prescribes penalty for them including hacking identity theft and cyber terrorism. It also facilitates Electronic Commerce by providing legal validity to electronic contracts and transactions. The act amended several times with significant changes in 2008 which introduce provisions for offensive messages, interception and monitoring of information. The act also established the controller of certifying authorities to regulate the issuance of digital signatures and a cyber appellate tribunals to resolve disputes.

CHAPTER TEN

# LAW FOR NGO LEADS TO RURAL DEVELOPMENT

Rural development involves the entire spectrum of activities intended to improve the lives of people who live in rural settings and to revitalize their economies and standard of living in the society. The organizations of civil society NGOs have been a vital part of this transition process, applying their know-how, resources and social network to solve the diversity of problems in rural areas. NGOs have utilized their resources to help bridge the gap and ensure that essential services and support find their way to the vulnerable. NGOs apply their know-how, resources and social network to solve the diversity of problems in rural areas. It deal with the sector, including agriculture, infrastructure, health, education, and social welfare. As NGOs represent the local needs of a community and the national policies, they act as the middle link between the solutions (government policies) and the problems that people in rural communities are experiencing (real world challenges). The NGOs, on their part, have become the inevitable partners in rural development, filling the gaps between government provisions and ground needs and bringing about positive changes in the lives of the rural communities. NGOs have proved their immense capabilities through innovative strategies and targeted interventions and remain committed. Therefore, NGOs can address the diverse challenges facing communities in rural areas. According to global changes, NGOs in rural development will be more important in future, thus the catalysts of a fairer and more sustainable world.

## *Key Areas of Focus for NGOs in Rural Development*

## *1. Agricultural Support and Sustainability*

NGOs perform a very important function of supporting and advancing sustainable farming methods, such as organic farming, crop diversification, and water management strategies. They do training, supply resources, and create market linkages to enhance farmers' productivity and farm incomes.

## *2. Healthcare Access and Improvement*

In communities where healthcare infrastructure often does not exist, NGOs have sought to give people access to clinics by introducing mobile services, improving sanitation facilities and supporting health education. They seek to promote consideration for the particular needs of healthcare provision in remote locations.

## *3. Educational Programs and Literacy*

NGOs are at the forefront of establishing community-based schools, technical training centres, as well as adult literacy centres in rural areas. To promote quality education, they reach out to rural communities and as a result, they empower them for social and economic development.

There are following laws which regulate formation and regulation of NGOs

1. Religious Endowment Act 1863
2. Trust Act 1882
3. Society Registration Act 1960
4. The Foreign Contribution (Regulation) Act, 2010
5. Companies Act 2013

# RELIGIOUS ENDOWMENT ACT 1863

The Religious Endowments Act, 1863 was enacted on 10th March 1863. It serves as a pivotal piece of legislation aimed at divesting government management and relieving the duties of Boards of Revenue concerning religious site

Religious Endowments Act, 1863 contains several key provisions:

1. Appointment of Commissioners: The act empowers the government to appoint commissioners to manage religious endowments. These commissioners oversee the administration of religious properties and funds.
2. Registration of Endowments: Religious endowments must be registered under this act. Registration ensures transparency and accountability in managing temple properties, funds, and assets.
3. Audit and Inspection: The act allows for regular audits and inspections of religious endowments. This ensures proper utilization of funds and prevents mismanagement.
4. Appointment of Trustees: The act outlines procedures for appointing trustees to manage religious properties. Trustees are responsible for maintaining temples, conducting rituals, and safeguarding endowment assets.
5. Powers of Commissioners: Commissioners have the authority to issue orders, settle disputes, and take necessary actions to protect endowments. They can also remove trustees for misconduct or negligence.

Remember that this act primarily applies to Hindu religious endowments

# TRUST ACT 1882

The Indian Trusts Act, 1882 governs private trusts established in India. Here are some key points:

1. Applicability: The Act applies to the entire country but excludes Waqf, mutual relations within an undivided family determined by customary or personal law, and religious or charitable endowments.
2. Definition of Trust: A trust involves the transfer of property by the owner (settlor) to another person (trustee) in whom the owner has confidence. The trustee holds the property for the benefit of a third person (beneficiary).
3. Objectives: Trusts should be created for lawful purposes. Section 4 of the Act outlines lawful purposes, including those that are not forbidden by law, fraudulent, immoral, or against public policy.
4. Creation: Any competent person (individual, AOP, HUF, company) can create a trust. If a minor is involved, permission from the Principal Civil Court of original jurisdiction is required.

# SOCIETY REGISTRATION ACT 1960

The Societies Registration Act of 1860 serves as a historical legal foundation for recognizing and governing societies involved in charitable, educational, or cultural activities. Its primary purpose is to formalize their existence and outline steps for proper functioning1. By facilitating registration, this act contributes to societal development and the promotion of noble causes.

Registering a society under the Societies Registration Act offers several advantages:

- Legal Recognition: Registration grants your society legal status, making it a separate legal entity. This recognition enables your society to own property, enter into contracts, and sue or be sued in its own name.
- Perpetual Existence: Unlike unregistered societies, registered ones continue to exist even if their members change. This ensures continuity and stability for your organization's goals.
- Credibility: Registered societies are perceived as more credible and trustworthy by donors, partners, and the public. This credibility can enhance fundraising efforts and collaborations.
- Tax Exemptions: Registered societies may qualify for tax exemptions on income and property. Consult local tax laws for specific details.
- Access to Grants and Funding: Many government and private agencies provide grants and funding exclusively to registered societies engaged in social, cultural, or educational activities

# THE FOREIGN CONTRIBUTION (REGULATION) ACT, 2010-

The Foreign Contribution (Regulation) Act, 2010 (FCRA) is a significant piece of legislation in India. Let me provide you with an overview:

1. Purpose and Scope:

- The FCRA aims to regulate the acceptance and utilization of foreign contributions or foreign hospitality by certain individuals, associations, or companies.
- It prohibits the acceptance and utilization of foreign contributions or hospitality for activities detrimental to national interest.

2. Applicability:

- The Act applies to associations (whether incorporated or not) having an office in India, including societies registered under the Societies Registration Act, 1860.
- It also covers citizens of India outside the country and associate branches or subsidiaries of Indian companies incorporated abroad.

3. Key Provisions:

- Prohibition on Acceptance: The Act prohibits the acceptance of foreign contributions unless registered under it.
- Restriction on Utilization: Foreign contributions cannot be used for administrative purposes beyond a specified limit.
- Political Organizations: There are specific procedures for notifying organizations of a political nature.
- Foreign Hospitality: Restrictions apply to accepting foreign hospitality.
- Transfer Restrictions: Foreign contributions cannot be transferred to other persons.

- Central Government's Powers: The government can prohibit receipt of foreign contributions in certain cases.
- Penalties and Offences: The Act outlines penalties for contravention of its provisions

# COMPANIES ACT 2013

Corporate Social Responsibility (CSR) is a self-regulating business model that encourages companies to be socially accountable to themselves, their stakeholders, and the public. By practicing CSR, also known as corporate citizenship, companies actively consider their impact on society and the environment. Rather than contributing negatively, they strive to enhance these aspects. CSR encompasses four main categories:

Environmental Responsibility: Companies focus on preserving the environment by reducing pollution, recycling materials, and replenishing natural resources. They may also create product lines consistent with CSR principles.

Ethical Responsibility: This involves fair treatment of customers, regardless of age, race, culture, or sexual orientation. It also includes favorable pay and benefits for employees, transparent disclosures, and ethical vendor relationships.

Philanthropic Responsibility: CSR requires companies to contribute to society. This can involve donating profits to charities, supporting employee philanthropic efforts, or sponsoring fundraising events.

Financial Responsibility: While planning environmentally, ethically, and philanthropically focused initiatives, companies must back these plans with financial investments in programs, research, and development.

CSR benefits both society and a company's brand image

SECTION 135 OF COMPANIES ACT 2013

135. Corporate Social Responsibility.—(1) Every company having net worth of rupees five hundred crore or more, or turnover of rupees one thousand crore or more or a net profit of rupees five crore or more during 2 [the immediately preceding financial year] shall constitute a Corporate Social Responsibility Committee of the Board consisting of three or more directors, out of which at least one director shall be an independent

director: 3 [Provided that where a company is not required to appoint an independent director under sub-section (4) of section 149, it shall have in its Corporate Social Responsibility Committee two or more directors.] (2) The Board's report under sub-section (3) of section 134 shall disclose the composition of the Corporate Social Responsibility Committee. (3) The Corporate Social Responsibility Committee shall,— (a) formulate and recommend to the Board, a Corporate Social Responsibility Policy which shall indicate the activities to be undertaken by the company 4 [in areas or subject, specified in Schedule VII]; (b) recommend the amount of expenditure to be incurred on the activities referred to in clause (a); and (c) monitor the Corporate Social Responsibility Policy of the company from time to time. (4) The Board of every company referred to in sub-section (1) shall,— (a) after taking into account the recommendations made by the Corporate Social Responsibility Committee, approve the Corporate Social Responsibility Policy for the company and disclose contents of such Policy in its report and also place it on the company's website, if any, in such manner as may be prescribed; and (b) ensure that the activities as are included in Corporate Social Responsibility Policy of the company are undertaken by the company. (5) The Board of every company referred to in sub-section (1), shall ensure that the company spends, in every financial year, at least two per cent. of the average net profits of the company made during the three immediately preceding financial years, 5 [or where the company has not completed the period of three financial years since its incorporation, during such immediately preceding financial years,] in pursuance of its Corporate Social Responsibility Policy: Provided that the company shall give preference to the local area and areas around it where it operates, for spending the amount earmarked for Corporate Social Responsibility activities: Provided further that if the company fails to spend such amount, the Board shall, in its report made under clause (o) of sub-section (3) of section 134, specify the reasons for not spending the amount 1. Subs. by Act 29 of 2020, s. 26, for sub-section (8) (w.e.f. 21-12-2020). 2. Subs. by Act 1 of 2018, s. 37, for "any financial year" (w.e.f. 19-9-2018). 3. The proviso ins. by s. 37, ibid., (w.e.f. 19-9-2018). 4. Subs. by s. 37, ibid., for "as specified in Schedule VII" (w.e.f. 19-9-2018). 5. Ins. by Act 22 of 2019, s. 21 (w.e.f. 22-1-2021). 94 1 [and, unless the unspent amount relates to any ongoing project referred to in sub-section (6), transfer such unspent amount to a Fund specified in Schedule VII, within a period of six months of the expiry of the financial years]. 2 [Provided also that if the company spends an amount in excess of the requirements provided under this sub-section, such company may set off such excess amount against the requirement to spend under this sub-section for such number of succeeding financial years and in such manner, as may be prescribed.] 3 [Explanation.—For the purposes of this section "net profit" shall not include such sums as may be prescribed, and shall be calculated in accordance with the provisions of section 198.] 4 [(6) Any amount remaining unspent under sub-section (5), pursuant to any ongoing project, fulfilling such conditions as may be prescribed, undertaken by a company in pursuance of its Corporate Social Responsibility Policy, shall be transferred by the company within a period of thirty days from the end of the financial year to a special account to be opened by the company in that behalf for that financial year in any scheduled bank to be called the Unspent Corporate Social Responsibility Account, and such amount shall be spent by the company in pursuance of its obligation towards the Corporate Social Responsibility Policy within a period of three financial years from the date of such transfer, failing which, the company shall transfer the same to a Fund specified in Schedule VII, within a period of thirty days from the date of completion of the third financial year. 5 [(7) If a company is in default in complying with the provisions of sub-section (5) or sub-section (6), the company shall be liable to a penalty of twice the amount required to be transferred by the company to the Fund specified in Schedule VII or the Unspent Corporate Social Responsibility Account, as the case may be, or one crore rupees, whichever is less, and every officer of the company who is in default shall be liable to a penalty of one-tenth of the amount required to be transferred by the company to such Fund specified in Schedule VII, or the Unspent Corporate Social Responsibility Account, as the case may be, or two lakh rupees, whichever is less.] (8) The Central Government may give such general or special directions to a company or class of companies as it considers necessary to ensure compliance of provisions of this section and such company or class of companies shall comply with such directions.] 6 [(9) Where the amount to be spent by a company under sub-section (5) does not exceed fifty lakh rupees, the requirement under sub-section (1) for constitution of the Corporate Social Responsibility Committee shall not be applicable and the functions of such Committee provided under this section shall, in such cases, be discharged by the Board of Directors of such company.]

CHAPTER ELEVEN

# LEADING CASES OF SUPREME COURT THE SUPREME COURT OF INDIA AGAINST SOCIAL EVIL

# a) Mrs. Githa Hariharan&Anr Vs. Reserve Bank of India &Anr. (AIR 1999, 2 SCC 228)

Bench: Anand CJI, Srinivasan J, Banerjee J

Date of Judgement: 17 February 1999

FACTS OF THE CASE

The petitioner and Dr. Mohan Ram were married at Bangalore in 1982 and in July 1984, a son named Rishab Bailey was born to them.

In December 1984 the petitioners applied to the Reserve Bank of India for 9% Relief Bond to be held in the name of their minor son Rishab along with an intimation that the petitioner No. 1 being the mother, would act as the natural guardian for the purpose of investments.

The application, however, was sent back to the petitioner by the RBI Authority advising her to produce the application signed by the father and in the alternative, the bank informed that a certificate of guardianship from a competent Authority in her favour.

Second, there was a divorce proceeding pending between the petitioner and her husband in which the husband prayed for the custody of the child.

In association with this, he had written many letters to the petitioner asserting that he is the natural guardian of the minor child and they could take no decision without his approval, which has resulted in the present case

Further the first respondent has been repeatedly writing to the petitioner, asserting that he was the only natural guardian of the minor and no decision should be taken without his permission. Incidentally, the minor has been staying with the mother. The father has shown total apathy towards the child and as a matter of fact, is not interested in welfare and benefit of the child excepting however claiming the right to be the natural guardian without however discharging any corresponding obligation.

It is on these facts that the petitioner moved this honorable court under Article 32 of the constitution praying for the declaration of Section 6(a) natural guardian of a Hindu minor read with Section 19(b)guardian not be appointed by the court in certain cases, under the light of Article 14 and 15 of the constitution of India as unconstitutional.

Two writ petitions one jointly by Githa Hariharan and her husband and another by Githa Hariharan alone herself was filed which was taken together by the ho'ble court.

Section 6 of the Hindu Minority and Guardianship Act (1956) and Section 19 of the Guardian and Wards Act (1890). The first of these acts says that the Hindu father is the "natural guardian" of his legitimate minor son and his minor unmarried daughter. He is the guardian of the child's "person and property" to the exclusion of the mother. The mother's rights enter the legal picture only if the father dies; takes to vanaprastha; turns yati or sanyasi; or if a court deems him "unfit" for guardianship. Section 19 of the Guardian and Wards Act debars the court from appointing the guardian of a minor whose father is living, and is not, in the court's opinion, unfit to be guardian.

LEGAL ISSUE:

Whether section 6 of the Hindu Minority and Guardianship Act violates the Constitution of India?

ARGUMENTS OFPETITIONER:

The main contention of Ms. Indira Jai Singh, learned senior counsel for the petitioners is that the two sections i.e. Section (6)a of HMG Act and Section 19(b) of GW Act are violative of the equality clause of the Constitution, inasmuch as the mother of the minor is relegated to an inferior position on ground of sex alone since her right, as a natural guardian of the minor, is made cognisable only `after' the father. Hence, according to the learned counsel both the sections must be struck down as unconstitutional.

1. The communication from the RBI is arbitrary and was opposed to the basic concept of justice under Article 32 of the constitution. Therefore challenging the validity of Section 6 of Hindu Minority and Wards Act, 1956.

2. Further, they argued that the provision seriously disadvantages women and discriminate against women in the matter of guardianship rights, responsibilities, and authority in relation to their own children.

JUDGEMENT:

On observing the facts and arguments the bench asserted the predominance of the child's welfare in all consideration. The welfare of the child is the most important over all the other, welfare not means only the monetary benefits, it includes love, affection, security, etc for the child. The bench pointed out the precedent Gajre vs. Pathnkhan. In which the father was alive, he was not taking any interest in the affairs of the child. In this case, the mother was ruled to be the natural guardian of her minor daughter. He set out that the Hindu law and the Act held that the father is the natural guardian and after him the mother but in the above cases, the court held the opposite.

In JijabaiVithalraoGajre Vs Pathankhan&Ors ..........a rigid insistence of strict statutory interpretation may not be conducive for the growth of the child, and welfare being the predominant criteria, it would be a planning exercise of the judicial power of interpreting the law so as to be otherwise conducive to a fuller and better development and growth of the child.

It was felt strongly that a long-established law should not easily be set aside; that a key point was an interpretation of the word "after" (Section 6 of Hindu Minority and Wards Act, 1956); and that,

...the word did not necessarily mean after the death of the father, on the contrary, it means 'in the absent off' be it temporary or otherwise or total apathy of the father towards the child or even inability of the father by reason of ailment or otherwise

The bench concluded that the literal meaning of the word [after] should not be taken, instead, it has to be interpreted to the object of the Act and the constitutional guarantee of gender equality since any other interpretation would render the statute void which ought to be avoided. Subsequently, the bench dismissed the petition with the direction to the Reserve Bank of India to formulate appropriate methodology in the light of his observations. The bench also instructed the District Court to take account of the comment when deciding the custody of the minor.

Conclusion :

From the facts, issues, and the decision of the apex court we learn that fighting for our rights is a vital part in our life. The power judicial review vested in the hand of the judiciary must be used properly without making any over-rule. Simply declaring any provision of an Act as unconstitutional or void is not the right way of judicial review, finding out the purpose of the provision under consideration is a vital part while deciding the constitutionality of any Act. From the decision of the above case, the judiciary plays its role in a proper and perfect manner.

KNOW YOUR CASE IN SHORT:

Githa Hariharan applied to the Reserve Bank of India for 9% Relief Bond to be held in the name of her minor son. RBI Authority advised her to produce the application signed by the father and in the alternative, the bank informed that a certificate of guardianship from a competent Authority in her favour as, as per Section 6 of Hindu Minority and Wards Act, 1956 she may not be considered as guardian as the father of the son is alive. Therefore for challenging the validity of Section 6 of Hindu Minority and Wards Act, 1956 read with Section 19 of the Guardian and Wards Act (1890) Section 19(b)guardian not be appointed by the court in certain cases, and declaring it as unconstituonal, she file a writ petition before Supreme Court. Hon'ble Supreme Cour pleased to dismiss the case with certain explanation and direction to the RBI about word 'after"

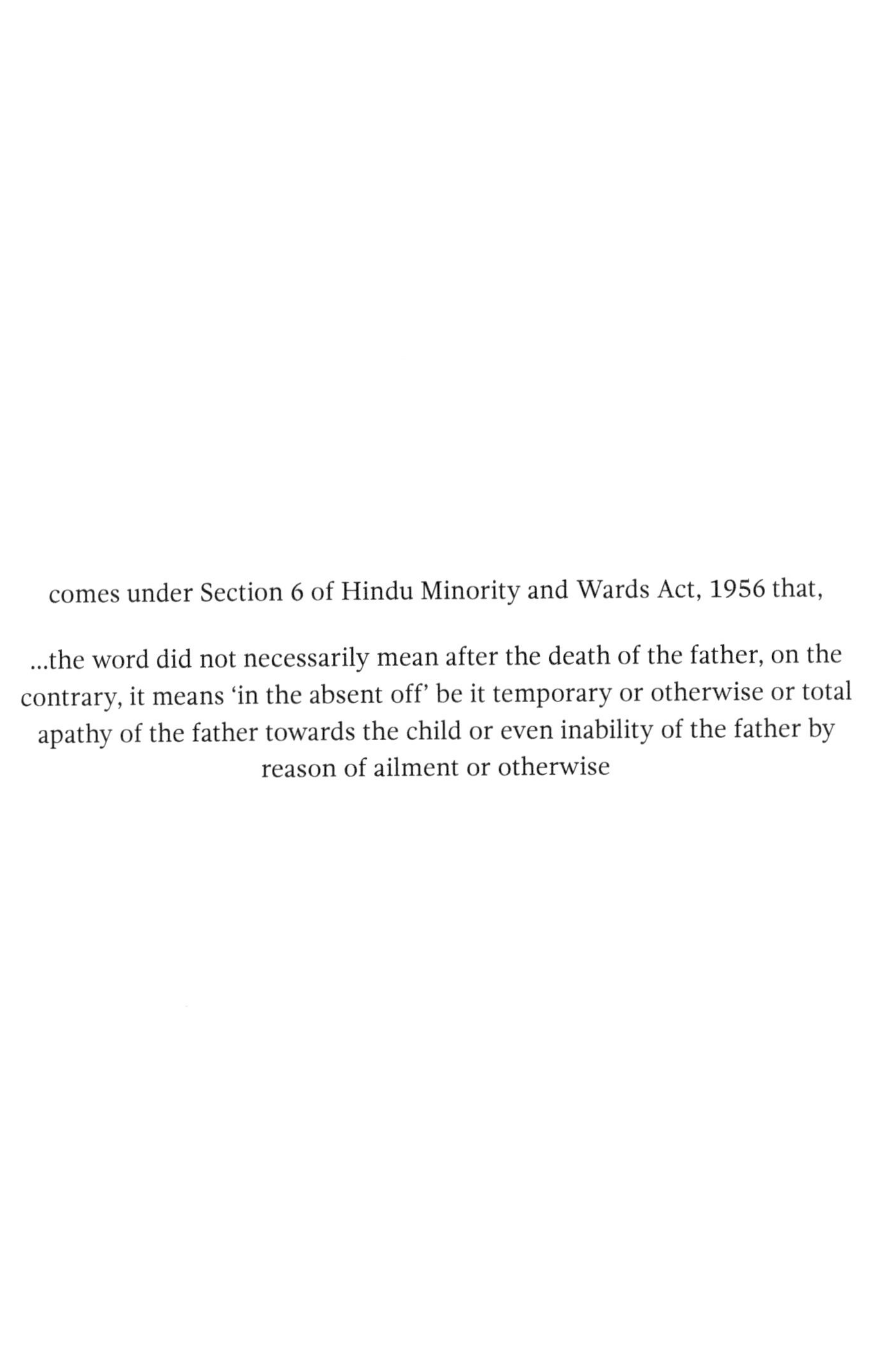

comes under Section 6 of Hindu Minority and Wards Act, 1956 that,

...the word did not necessarily mean after the death of the father, on the contrary, it means 'in the absent off' be it temporary or otherwise or total apathy of the father towards the child or even inability of the father by reason of ailment or otherwise

# b) Shayara Bano vs. Union of India & Ors. [2017] 9SCR 797 : (2017) 9 SCC 1

(The three judges in the majority regarded triple talaq invalid, but used different reasoning to arrive at their conclusion: Justices Rohington Nariman and U. U. Lalit held that the 1937 Muslim Personal Law (Shariat) Application Act, in so far as it refers to triple talaq, violated Article 14 of the Indian constitution - the right to equality. Justice Kurian Joseph held that triple talaq was not a valid practice in Islam and was therefore illegal.)

CORAM : Justices Khehar, Justice Nazeer, Justices Nariman and Justices Lalit & Justice Joseph

LEGAL BACKGROUND IN THE CASE :

The practice of Triple Talaq promotes cruelty towards women. It promotes exploitation. It shows how a man recklessly ends the marriage on his whims. It is not the first time that a judgement has been made on Triple Talaq –

in the case DagduLatur vs. RahimbDagdu Pathan, 2002 Bombay High Court - It was held by the full bench that 9 "a Muslim husband cannot dissolve a marriage at will and for triple talaq to be valid the facts of the due talaq procedure should be proved in court."

Case of Shamim Ara vs. State of U.P. &Anr -: Invalidate the arbitrary triple talaq, It was held by SC that the facts which lead to talaq must be proven and just a document stating the date or events of talaq will not be considered as the valid talaq.

Masroor Ahmed vs. State (NCT of Delhi) &Anr. - Holding the instant talaq as invalid, it was held by the Delhi High Court that "..where a talaq is revocable, the attempts at reconciliation can take place even after the pronouncement. This is so, because, in a revocable talaq, the dissolution of marriage does not take place at the time of pronouncement but is automatically deferred till the end of the iddat period." It raises the question whether can we, in under the cover of personal law, attack the rights of women? Another point to mention is that, nowhere in Hadis or Quran the practice of Triple Talaq is mentioned. It has been the matter of innovation by which people made a distorted law for selfish and thoughtless purposes without caring what consequences a woman will have to face.

FACTS OF THE CASE :

1. In the case of Sarabai v. Rabaibai5, 5 years before the Muslim Personal Law (Sharait) Act 1937, the court held that "it is a good law but bad is ideology". For the next two decades there were different judgments which came out for and against this custom. One of the most significant being Shamin Aru v. State of Uttar Pradesh8 in 2002 where the conditions for a valid talaq were mentioned. Although it did not deal with the triple talaq directly it however did spark a discussion of what counts as a valid talaq. This case was future used as a binding precedent later on as to why triple talaq is invalid.

2. The decision at hand brought together five writ petitions filed by Muslim women who had been divorced by way of triple talaq. Among them was the petitioner who gave the case its name, ShayaraBano, a 35-year old women, who has two children from her marriage and was divorced by her husband in October 2015 after 15 years of marriage.

3. ShayaraBano, a woman survivor of domestic violence and dowry harassment had been unilaterally divorced through Triple Talaq(Talaq-E-Idat). She filed a Writ Petition before the Supreme Court seeking a declaration that the practices of Triple Talaq, polygamy, and Nikah Halala in Muslim personal law were illegal, unconstitutional, and in violation of Articles 14 (equality before law), 15 (non-discrimination), 21 (right to life with dignity) and 25 (right to freedom of conscience and religion) of the Indian Constitution. The Court however chose to examine the issue of Triple Talaq alone.

4. Talaq-e- bidat is a practise which gives a man the right to divorce his wife by uttering 'talaq' three times in one sitting without his wife's consent. Nikah Halala is a practise where a divorced woman who wants to remarry her husband would have to marry and obtain a divorce, from a second husband before she can go back to her first husband. And polygamy is a practice which allows Muslim men to have more than one wife.

5. Muslim women's groups - the Bharatiya Muslim MahilaAndolanand Bebak Collective - intervened in the matter to support the petitioners. A key player defending the practice of triple talaq was the All India Muslim Personal Law Board (AIMPLB). The court directed the registration of a public interest litigation (PIL) case, entitled In Re: Muslim Women's Quest For Equality vs JamiatUlma-I-Hind. The deliberative decision to put five judges of five different religious communities, namely a Sikh, a Christian, a Parsi, a Hindu and a Muslim (all male) on the bench to decide this case was clearly an attempt not to repeat the mistakes made in Shah Banoand possibly also a signal to the Muslim community that their concerns were being taken seriously and that the case would be looked at in the most objective manner.

6. It is important to note that though the petition mentions several judgments which have dealt with the triple talaqconundrum it does not rely on the ratio of any of the judgements but rather challenges the constitutional validity of the triple talaq. Further the petition discussed that as triple talaqis not an essential tenet of the religious belief of the Muslims it is not saved by article 25 of the Constitution of India. However the petition nowhere questions the inherent discretion given to the Muslim husband to pronounce talaqto the wife, rather it onlychallenges the practice of triple talaq. Hence the ShayaraBano petition does not bring out the ills of triple talaq it stands today.

ISSUES FRAMED :

1. Whether the practice of talaq-e-bidat (specifically - instantaneous triple talaq) an essential practice of Islam?

2. Whether the practice of Triple Talaq violates any fundamental right ?

ARGUMENT OF PETITIONER :

1. Triple talaq violated fundamental rights, namely Articles 14, 15 and 21. With reference to Masilamani Mudaliar as well as other cases in which the Supreme Court has tested the personal laws on the touchstone of fundamental rights, it was opined that Muslim personal law should be considered as "law in force" within the meaning of Article 13(1).

2. Triple talaq is arbitrary and discriminatory and thus a violation of Articles 14 and 15. As held in Kesavananda Bharati and Minerva Mills, it was the courts‘ duty to intervene in cases of violation of any individual's fundamental right, and to render justice.

3. This was even more so in cases where the parliament was reluctant in bringing out legislation - presumably due to political considerations. It was further held that the Constitution's provisions on religious freedom did not in any manner impair the jurisdiction of the Court. Article 25 itself postulated that religious freedom was subject to other provisionsin part III. Articles 14 and 15, on the other hand, were not subject to any restrictions.

4. Triple talaq was in fact not even protected by Article 25, because it would not form an "essential practice" of religion.

5. international treaties and covenants to which India is a party, such as the Universal Declaration of Human Rights, the International Covenant on Economic Social and Cultural Rights, and the Convention on the Elimination of All Forms of Discrimination Against Women and the respective references to gender equality, non-discrimination and human dignity therein.

6. It was held that triple talaq was not in tune with the prevailing social conditions, as Muslim women were vociferously protesting against the practice. It was held that triple talaq should be abolished in the same manner as the state had done away with practices once prevalent in the

Hindu community, such as sati, devdasi and polygamy. The fact that a number of countries, including theocratic states and countries with large Muslim majorities, had prohibited triple talak.

JUDGMENT :

MAJORITY OPINION :

The three judges in the majority regarded triple talaq invalid, but used different reasoning to arrive at their conclusion: Justices Rohington Nariman and U. U. Lalit held that the 1937 Muslim Personal Law (Shariat) Application Act, in so far as it refers to triple talaq, violated Article 14 of the Indian constitution - the right to equality. Justice Kurian Joseph held that triple talaq was not a valid practice in Islam and was therefore illegal.

The first question was decided in different ways by the different judges. Justices Nariman and Lalit held that the 1937 Act did indeed codify tripletalaq under statutory law. They held that "all forms of Talaq recognized and enforced by Muslim personal law are recognized and enforced by the 1937 Act. This would necessarily include Triple Talaq". As a pre-constitutional law, the 1937 Act would fall within the expression "laws in force" and would be "hit by Article 13(1) if found to be inconsistent with the provisions in Part III of the Constitution"

Justice Joseph answered this question in the negative, while Justices Khehar and Nazeer answered it in the positive.Justice Joseph stated:"Merely because a practice has continued for long, that by itself cannot make it valid if it has been expressly declared to be impermissible" (para 24) and concluded: "What is held to be bad in the Holy Quran cannot be good in Shariat and, in that sense, what is bad in religion is bad in law as well"

Justices Nariman and Lalit, who had regarded triple talaqas codified into statutory law by the 1937 Act and thus subject to fundamental rightsscrutiny, the next question was whether Section 2 of the 1937 Act, to the extent that it authorisedtriple talaq, actually violated any constitutional provisions and was therefore insofarunconstitutional and void. Before engaging with a violation of Article 14, the justices -in a similar vein to Justices Khehar and Nazeer above - proved whether triple talaq was"saved" by Article 25.

Justice Nariman and Lalit denied such a saving through Article 25. They argued instead that triple talaq - which was perceivedas sinful in theology - did not constitute an "essential religious practices" and wastherefore not protected under Article 25(1) (para 25). The judges held that there was noneed that "the ball must be bounced back to the legislature" (para 25), and that the courtcould decide on the matter. The Supreme Court's judgement in the Ahmedabad Women ActionGroup case36 was in this context dismissed as having "no ratio" and being contradictoryin itself (para 30).Having said this, the judges engaged with the core issue of the case: the question ofwhether the 1937 Act, insofar as it seeks to enforce triple talaq, was a violation of any constitutionalprovision, in this case Article 14. With extensive reference to the SupremeCourt's jurisprudence, the judges argued that "legislation can be struck down on the groundthat it is arbitrary and, therefore, violative of Article 14 of the Constitution" (para 54). This"test of manifest arbitrariness" was then applied to the case at hand. Since triple talaq wasvalid without any "reasonable cause" and did not allow for "any attempt at reconciliationbetween the husband and wife" (para 56), the judges concluded that:"this form of Talaq is manifestly arbitrary in the sense that the marital tie can be brokenunpredictably and creatively by a Muslim man without any attempt at reconciliationso as to save it. This form of talaq must, therefore, be held to be violative of thefundamental right contained under Article 14 of the Constitution of India. In ouropinion, therefore, the 1937 Act, insofar as it seeks to recognize and enforce TripleTalaq, is within the meaning of the expression 'laws in force' in Article 13(1) andmust be struck down as being void to the extent that it recognizes and enforces TripleTalaq" (para 57).

MINORITY OPINION :

1. The minority view, held by Chief Justice Jagdish Singh Khehar and Justice Abdul Nazeer, was that though triple talaq was undesired, the

courts could not strike it down, and only the parliament could regulate on the matter. The judgement is a landmark case in the Indian women's movement's agitating for more rights under religion based personal laws.

2. On the other hand, contrary to the fundamentalrights in part III of the constitution, directive principles in part IV such as Article 44 are not enforceable by the court (see Article 37). They do not directly create any justiciable rights in favour of individuals, nor can a law be declared unconstitutional on the sole ground that it contravenes a directive principle. However here things become a little more interesting - Article 13(1) provides that "[all laws in force in the territory of India immediately before the commencement of this Constitution, in so far as they are inconsistent with the provisions of this Part [part III – the fundamental rights], shall, to the extent of such inconsistency, be void".

3. The fundamental rights in part III of the constitution include the right to equality, enshrined in Articles 14 (equality before the law) and 15 (no discrimination on grounds of religion, race, caste, sex or place of birth) as well as the right to life, guaranteed under Article 21 (generally interpreted in a broad sense as including personal liberty and the right to live with human dignity11). Interestingly, in 1952, in the case NarasuAppa Mali12 the Bombay High Court held that (uncodified) "personal laws were not included in the expression 'laws in force' used in Article 13(1)" (para 13). Consequently, the court held that (uncodified) personal laws were not void even when they came into conflict with the provision of equality under the constitution. While the Indian Supreme Court has never directly overruled this judgement.

4. Justices Khehar and Nazeer, on the other hand, regarded triple talaq as a part of uncodified Muslim personal law and consequently had to answer whether or not the same could be tested against the constitution by the court. The two justices answered this question in the negative. This was because, in their opinion, the personal laws of any religious community were "protected from invasion and breach, except as provided by and under Article 25" (para 146).

5. This interpretation in particular has been criticised, as it regards a law rather than an individual as being protected under Article 25. The justices did not see a reason to engage with the relationship between Articles 25 vis-à-vis Articles 14, 15 and 21 as "other provisions of this part", which the freedom of religion is "subject to" (Article 25(1)), as they held that these rights were only applicable to State action against individuals (para 165). They concluded that the court "cannot nullify and declare as unacceptable in law, what the constitution decrees us, not only to protect, but also to enforce. Article 25 obliges all Constitutional Courts to protect 'personal laws' and not to find fault therewith. Interference in matters of 'personallaw' is clearly beyond judicial examination" (para 195). The judges "direct, the Union of India to consider appropriate legislation, particularly with reference to 'talaq-e-biddat'"(para 199).
Overall, though via a different argumentation, Justices Nariman and Lalit thereby came to the same conclusion as Justice Kurian Joseph and by a majority of 3:2 the practice of tripletalaq was set aside.

# c) Shakti Vahini vs. Union of India & Ors. [2018] 3 SCR 770 : (2018) 7 SCC 192

(In the case of Shakti Vahini v Union of India, the court laid down guidelines that need to be implemented by the government for the eradication of Honour killing in India. An honour killing is the homicide of a member of a family by other members, due to the perpetrators having the belief that the victim violated the principles of a community or a religion the victim has brought shame or dishonour upon the family.)

Citation: WRITE PETITION (CIVIL) NO. 231 OF 2010

CORAM : CJI Dipak Misra J. A.M. Khanwilkar J. Dr. D.Y. Chandrachud.

Date of Judgement: 27 March 2018.

FACTS OF THE CASE :

1. A Writ Petition by NGO Shakti Vahini has been preferred under Article 32 of the Constitution of India seeking directions to the respondents-State Governments and the Central Government to take preventive steps to combat honour crimes, to submit a National Plan of Action and State Plan of Action to curb crimes of the said nature and further to direct the State Governments to constitute special cells in each district which can be approached by the couples for their safety and well being.

2. That apart, prayers have been made to issue a writ of mandamus to the State Governments to launch prosecutions in each case of honour killing and take appropriate measures so that such honour crimes and embedded evil in the mindset of certain members of the society are dealt with iron hands.

3. The petitioner-organization was authorized for conducting Research Study on "Honour Killings in Haryana and Western Uttar Pradesh" by order dated 22.12.2009 passed by the National Commission for Women. It is averred that there has been a spate of such honour killings in Haryana,

Punjab and Western Uttar Pradesh and the said trend is on the increase and such killings have sent a chilling sense of fear amongst young people who intend to get married but do not enter into wedlock out of fear. The social pressure and the consequent inhuman treatment by the core groups who arrogate to themselves the position of law makers and impose punishments which are extremely cruel instill immense fear that compels the victims to commit suicide or to suffer irreparably at the hands of these groups.

ISSUES :

1. Whether an individual has a right to choose life partner of his/her choice?

2. Whether honour killings undertaken by khap panchayats are legal ?

ARGUMENTS OF PETITIONER :

1. It was contended by petitioners that because IPC does not appropriately deal with honour killing. Khap panchayats do not feel guilt or hesitation in committing such crimes.

2. It was submitted that honour takes precedence over the choice of two consenting adults, and they are subject to inhuman behaviour for expressing their choice.

3. These extra constitutional Bodies which engage in feudalistic activities have no compunction to commit such crimes which are offences under the Indian Penal Code.

4. Article 21 which provides for protection of life and personal liberty and guard basic human rights and equality of status has not been taken care of by these bodies. The crimes like honour killings are a violation of Article 21.

ARGUMENTS OF RESPONDANT :

1. Honour Killings are treated as murder as defined under Section 300 of the IPC and punishable under Section 302 of the IPC. As the police and public order are state subjects under the Constitution, it is primarily the responsibility of the states to deal with honour killings.

2. Central Government is engaging various States and Union Territories for considering a proposal to either amend the IPC or enact a separate legislation to address this menace.

3. Since the matter of the 242nd law commission report falls under list 3 i.e. Concurrent list of the seventh schedule to the Constitution of India, consultation with the governments of the states and UTs is a sine qua non for taking a policy decision in this regard. It is also submitted that it is considering the'The prohibition of interference with the Freedom of Matrimonial Alliance Bill' recommended by this Law Commission.

4. Although some states have formed an action plan in the name in pursuance of the directions issued by this court, yet they have failed to effectively implement the same in letter and spirit. And so effective guidelines to the police and law enforcement agencies to curb the menace of honour killing need to be formulated and implemented.

COURT FURTHER RELIED ON SEVERAL CASES :

In Lata Singh vs State of U.P, the court observed that there is no bar for inter-caste marriage under the Hindu Marriage Act or any other law. Court further held that this is a free and democratic country, and once a person becomes a major he or she can marry whosoever he /she likes.

In Re: India Woman says Gang-raped on Orders of Village Court published in Business, court held that the State is duty-bound to protect the fundamental rights of its citizens; and an inherent aspect of Article 21 of the Constitution would be the freedom of choice in marriage. Such offences are resultant of the State's incapacity or inability to protect the fundamental rights of its citizens.

In Asha Ranjan v. State of Bihar and others, the Court noted that the choice of woman in choosing her partner in life is a legitimate constitutional right. It is founded on individual choice that is recognised in the Constitution under Article 19, and such a right is not expected to succumb to the concept of"class honour" or"group thinking" .

In Kartar Singh V. State of Punjab, the court held, Honour killing hinders individual liberty, freedom of choice and one's own perception of choice. When two adults make arrive at a consensual decision to marry each other, it is an expression of their choice which is recognized under Articles 19 & 21 of the Constitution. Such a right is recognized under the constitution and hence needs to be protected from the illegitimate conception of class honour or group thinking.

In Arumugam Servai vs. State of Tamil Nadu, the court directed the administration and police officials to take strong measures to prevent such atrocious acts. Further the State Government was directed to institute criminal proceedings against those responsible for the acts and to suspend the District Magistrate/Collector and SSP/SPs of the district as well as other officials concerned and charge sheet them

JUDGMENT :

1. The court in this case observed: Two consenting adults do not need the consent of their families and elders to get married. Further, any attempt of the Khap panchayat or any other body to suppress their wishes to marry each other is illegal. The court observes: "Class honour, howsoever perceived cannot smother the choice of an individual which he or she is entitled to enjoy under our compassionate constitution "

2. Referring to the 242$^{nd}$ report of the Law Commission, the SC highlighted the devastating impact is not the only type of crime ordered by Khap panchayat. It is a part of honour-based crimes. Any type of honour-based crime which is meant to suppress an individual's choice to love marriage is illegal.

3. Reliance was also placed on ArumgamServai v. State of Tamil Nadu, to hold that Honour Killing in this sense violates individual liberty and freedom of choice (para 42)

DIRECTIVES ISSUED BY THE COURT :

Preventive measures

1. State govt. are requested to identify areas where incidents killings or assembly of Kaph panchayats have been reported in the last 5 years

2. The superintendents of police in these areas are required to be more vigilant in case of inter-religion or inter-caste marriages taking place in the area.

3. If a police officer comes to know of any gathering of Khap panchayat taking place in the area, should inform his superior officer as well as Deputy/ Superintendent of Police.

4. On receipt of such information, DSP/SP is required to be present and he shall inform the members that they are not to take any decision to harm the couple or their family. If such a decision is taken each member will be criminally liable.

5. If after interacting with members of the Khap, DSP has reason to believe that the meeting cannot be prevented or the couple is likely to be harmed, then he can report to the DM/SDM asking to issue order u/s 144, 151 CrPC.

6. Home department and state govt. are required to work together to sensitise the law enforcement agencies stakeholders in this process. There should be institutional machinery to coordinate with all stakeholders.

Remedial Measures

1. Despite the preventive measures, the Khap panchayat passes any verdict against a couple an FIR should be registered.

2. Police are also directed to take the effective investigation of the charge made in the FIR and provide protection to the couple/family and also if necessary organise their marriage with police protection.

3. State govt. to make provision of 'safe houses' for such couples.

4. On receipt of a complaint from a couple/family that any khap panchayat is opposing their marriage, the DM/SP shall entrust an Addl. SP with a duty to conduct a preliminary investigation to ascertain the authenticity, nature and gravity of the threat. On being satisfied as to the authenticity of the threat he is required to submit a report to the S.P.

4. Failure by police or district officials to comply with the above directions shall be considered as an act of deliberate negligence or misconduct for which departmental action must be initiated and concluded within 6 months.

5. Disciplinary action will be taken against officials who knew (i). about the incident but did not prevent or (ii). where such incident had occurred, they did not respond promptly (Arumugam Servai v. State of TN).

6. Special cells and 24-hour helplines must be created.

7. Speedy trails for cases relating to honour killings and violence against couples. These cases must be concluded within 6 months, this direction also applies to pending cases.

# d) NAVTEJ SINGH JOHAR & ORS. VERSUS UNION OF INDIA THR. SECRETARY MINISTRY OF LAW AND JUSTICE [2018] 7 SCR 379 : (2018) 10 SCC 1

(Decriminalised Homosexuality- five-judge Bench consisting then Chief Justice Dipak Mishra, Justice A.M. Khanwilkar, Justice D.Y. Chandrachud, Justice R.F. Nariman and Justice Indu Malhotra. Four separate judgments were delivered wherein the court partially struck down Section 377 of the Indian Penal Codeunanimously struck downSection 377 of the Indian Penal Code, to the extent that it criminalised same-sex relations between consenting adults. LGBT individuals are now legally allowed to engage in consensual intercourse. The Court upheld provisions in Section 377 that criminalise non-consensual acts or sexual acts performed on animals.)

On 6$^{th}$ September 2018

CORAM : five-judge Bench consisting then Chief Justice Dipak Mishra, Justice A.M. Khanwilkar, Justice D.Y. Chandrachud, Justice R.F. Nariman and Justice Indu Malhotra.

BACKGROUND / FACTS OF THE CASE :

1. Section 377 of the Indian Penal Code (IPC) criminalised consensual sexual intercourse between persons of the same sex for being "against the order of nature".

2. In 2009, before the Delhi High Court, the Naz Foundation (India) Trust challenged the constitutionality of Section 377 for violating Articles 14, 15, 19 and 21 of the Constitution. The court ruled that punishing sexual activity between two consenting adults under Section 377 violates the right to equality, privacy and personal liberty of such persons.

3. This decision was appealed before the Supreme Court and in 2013, the Court reversed the Naz verdict in Suresh Kumar Koushal & Anr. v. Naz Foundation & Ors. ("Koushal"). It held that only the Parliament could decriminalise homosexualit.

4. Five individuals from the LGBTQ communities (Navtej Singh Johar, Ritu Dalmia, Ayesha Kapur, Aman Nath and Sunil Mehra) filed a new writ petition challenging the constitutionality of Section 377.

## ISSUES :

1. The Court deliberated on the soundness of the Koushal decision. It also considered whether Section 377 violates:

a) Article 14 as it discriminates against individuals on the basis of their "sexual orientation" and "gender identity"?

b) The right to autonomy and dignity under Article 21 by penalizing private consensual acts between same-sex persons?

c) The right to expression under Article 19(1)(a) by criminalising the gender expression of the LGBTQI+ community?

## ARGUMENTS OF PETITIONER :

1. Homosexuality, bisexuality or any other sexual interest is something natural and is not a physical or mental illness. It is a reflection of personal choice and criminalising it will lead to the destructing of Article 21 of the Indian Constitution by affecting an individuals dignity and his or her gender identity.

2. It is also argued that a person will not become an alien if his community is not accepted by the society at large and therefore rights of the LGBT community who constitutes 7-8% of Indian population needs to be recognised.

3. Section-377 is based on the morals and social values of Victorian-era where sexual activities were just considered as a reproductive process and

nothing more than that. This section is the only reason that the LGBT community has suffered discrimination and abuse all their lives and will continue to suffer if homosexuality is criminalised again.

4. If section-377 is retained in without making any amendments then it would lead to the violation of various fundamental rights of the LGBT group i.e. right to freedom of expression, right to privacy, right to equality, liberty and dignity.

5. Petitioners have also mentioned that people who choose inter-religious and inter-caste marriages are the same as people who choose a partner of same-sex and there is no difference between them. Society may or may not disapprove of inter-caste and inter-religious marriages but it is the duty of the court to enforce constitutional rights of every citizen. Position of the LGBT group is the same, even though the majority is disapproving them but it is to the court to protect their constitutional rights from being violated.

6. There is no reasonable classification between natural and unnatural sex and even the expression "carnal intercourse against the order of nature" is not defined anywhere. Therefore section-377 is arbitrary and vague and is violative of Article 14.

7. The section is also violative of Article 15 as it discriminates the LGBT community on the basis of sex of their partners which is prohibited under Article 15 of the Indian Constitution.

ARGUMENTS OF RESPONDANT :

1. It has been submitted by them if section-377 is declared as unconstitutional then the family system will be destroyed and many corrupt young Indians will see this as a trade and will start using homosexual activities for money. Moreover, individuals indulging in such activities are more likely to contract HIV/AIDS which will increase the percentage of AIDS victim in the country.

2. It is also contended that the political, economic and cultural heritage of countries were consensual homosexual acts have been decriminalised are very much different from a multicultural and diverse country like India.

3. Fundamental rights are not absolute and decriminalising section-377 will leave all the religions practised in the country as objectionable and will lead to the violation of Article 25 of Indian Constitution which also needs to be given due consideration.

4. They also submitted that clarifications can be added to section-377 by defining every word which is controversially mentioned in the section. The section will then target people with mollified intentions and non-consensual acts.

5. The main reason behind criminalising carnal intercourse against nature is to protect the citizens from the injurious consequences as protecting the citizens from something hazardous is one of the aims of criminal law.

6. Article 15 prohibits discrimination on the basis of sex but not on sexual orientation, therefore section-377 of IPC is not violating Article 15. Moreover, it is also not violative of Article 14 as the section only mentions a particular offence along with its punishment.

JUDGMENT :

All five judges overruled Koushal. The Court drew on the doctrine of progressive realisation of rights to hold that rights should not be revoked. The march of a progressive society should only be forward.

The Court also noted the guarantee of a fundamental right to privacy in Justice K.S. Puttaswamy Vs UOI and held that Koushal's finding that Section 377 affected only a 'minuscule minority' cannot be the basis to deny the right to privacy. It observed that minorities face discrimination because their views and beliefs do not align with the majority and the Koushal decision violated the right of all persons to equal protection.

Five-judge Bench partially struck down Section 377 of the Indian Penal Code, decriminalising same-sex relations between consenting adults. LGBT individuals are now legally allowed to engage in consensual intercourse. The Court has upheld provisions in Section 377 that criminalise non-consensual acts or sexual acts performed on animals.The Supreme Court tested the constitutionality of Section 377 against the principles of equality, liberty, dignity under Articles 14, 19 and 21

1. Right to Equality and Non-Discrimination:The Court observed that Section 377 arbitrarily punishes individuals who engage in same sex relationships. To substantiate this, the Court noted that Section 377 classifies and punishes individuals who engage in carnal intercourse against the order of nature to protect women and children. However, this objective has no reasonable nexus with the classification, as unnatural offences have also been separately penalised under Section 375 and the POCSO Act. Therefore, the Court held that the unequal treatment of LGBT individuals violates Article 14.Further, the Court held that Section 377 is manifestly arbitrary as it does not distinguish between consensual and non-consensual sexual acts between adults. It targeted people exercising certain choices and treated them as "less than humans" and encouraged prejudices and stereotypes accompanied by debilitating social effects. This violates Article 14, which is the very basis of non-discrimination.

2. Freedom of Expression:The Court acknowledged that all persons, including LGBTQI individuals, had the right to express their choices without any fear. It recognised same-sex sexuality as a normal variant of human sexuality. In particular, the Court noted that Section 377 stigmatises and discriminates against transgender persons.Next, the Court tested whether public order, decency and morality are reasonable grounds to restrict the right to freedom of expression of sexuality under Article 19(1)(a). It noted that Section 377 criminalises private consensual acts which neither disturb public order, nor injure public decency or morality. Sexual acts cannot be viewed solely from the lens of morality where they are seen to be purely for procreation. An unreasonable restriction on acts within a person's private space will have a chilling effect on freedom of choice.For these reasons, the Court held that Section 377 is

disproportionate and violates the fundamental right to freedom of expression.

3. Right to Life and Personal Liberty:The Court held that Section 377 violates human dignity, decisional autonomy and the fundamental right to privacy. Every individual has the liberty to choose their sexual orientation, seek companionship and exercise it within their private space. As Section 377 inhibits the exercise of personal liberty to engage in voluntary sexual acts, it violates Article 21. It socially ostracises LGBT persons and does not permit full realisation of their personhood.Denying the right to determine one's sexual orientation curtails the right to privacy of an individual. Therefore, the Court held that the scope of the right to privacy must be widened to incorporate and protect 'sexual privacy'.

In this way Court upheld the right to equal citizenship of all members of the LGBTQI community in India. Thus, it read down Section 377 to exclude consensual sexual relationships between adults, whether between same-sex individuals or otherwise. Section 377 will continue to apply to non-consensual sexual activity against adults, sexual acts against minors and bestiality.

# e) Joseph Shine vs. Union of India [2018] 11 SCR 765: (2019) 3 SCC 39

(Adultery as a criminal offence has no significance because it is a private matter in which courts should not interfere. There is sexual autonomy to every individual and hindering the same would violate the constitutional principles. This judgement decriminalizes the offence of adultery and makes it a ground for civil wrongs only. Criminalizing both men and women as suggested by Law Commission reports would not have served the purpose as adultery is an act which is an extremely private affair related to the matrimonial realm.)

Date of decision: 27th September 2018

CORAM : Chief Justice Dipak Misra, justice A. Khanwilkar, justice R. F. Nariman, justice D. Y. Chandrachud, justice Indu Malhotra

BACKGROUND OF THE CASE :

Adultery in India was based on the notion of patriarchy and male chauvinism. This offence makes a man criminally liable who has sexual relations with a woman, who is the wife of another man. And if the husband consents or connives to such an act it will no longer be adultery.

There is no right to a woman in case her husband commits adultery. In ancient history, adultery was considered to be a sinful act either done by a married man or woman.

Adultery in India does not treat a woman as a culprit but as a victim who has been seduced by a man to do such an act. This law is violative of our constitutional principles i.e. equality, non-discrimination, right to live with dignity and so on.

Adultery has been struck down as an offence in as many as 60 countries including South Korea, South Africa, Uganda, Japan etc., on being gender discriminative and violating the right to privacy. Even Lord Macaulay, the creator of the penal code objected its presence in the penal code as an offence rather suggested that it should be better left as a civil wrong.

The law evolves with the time and many recent judgements have increased the ambit of fundamental rights in conformity with changing societal values and increasing individual liberty. This judgement joins them in creating history by striking down 158-year-old law which has lost its relevance with changing social and moral conditions.

## FACTS OF THE CASE :

A writ petition was filed under Article 32 by Joseph Shine challenging the constitutionality of Section 497 of IPC read with Section 198 of Cr. P.C., being violative of Article 14, 15 and 21. This was at first a PIL filed against adultery.

2. The petitioner claimed the provision for adultery to be arbitrary and discriminatory on the basis of gender. The petitioner claimed that such a law demolishes the dignity of a woman. The constitutional bench of 5 judges was set up to hear the petition.

## ISSUES :

1. Whether the provision for adultery is arbitrary and discriminatory under Article 14?

2. Whether the provision for adultery encourages the stereotype of women being the property of men and discriminates on gender basis under Article15?

3. Whether the dignity of a woman is compromised by denial of her sexual autonomy and right to self-determination?

4. Whether criminalizing adultery is intrusion by law in the private realm of an individual?

## ARGUMENT OF PETITIONER :

1. That the provision criminalizes adultery on classification based on sex alone which has no rational nexus to object to being achieved. The consent of the wife is immaterial. Hence violative of Article 14 of the constitution.

2. The provision is based on the notion that a woman is property of the husband. The provision says if the husband gives consent or connive then adultery is not committed.

3. The provision for adultery is discriminative on the basis of gender as it provides only men with the right to prosecute against adultery which is violative of Article 15.

4. The petitioner contended that the provision is unconstitutional as it undermines the dignity of a woman by not respecting her sexual autonomy and self-determination. It is violative of Article 21 and therefore Section 497 of IPC read with Section 198 of CrPC must be struck down.

ARGUMENT OF RESPONDENT :

1. The adultery is an offence which breaks the family relations and deterrence should be there to protect the institution of marriage.

2. The respondents claim that adultery affects the spouse, children and society as a whole. It is an offence committed by an outsider with full knowledge to destroy the sanctity of marriage.

3. The discrimination by the provision is saved by Article 15(3), which provides state right to make special laws for women and children.

They request the court to delete the portion found unconstitutional but retain the provision.

PREVIOUS JUDGMENT :

Yusuf Abdul Aziz vs. State of Bombay (1954) SCR 930

In this case, the constitutionality of Section 497 was challenged on the grounds that it violates Article 14 and Article 15, by saying a wife cannot be a culprit even as an abettor. The 3 judge bench upheld the validity of the said provision as it is a special provision created for women and is saved by Article 15(3). And Article 14 is a general provision and has to be read with other Articles and sex is just classification, so by combining both it is valid.

Sowmithri Vishnu v. Union of India &Anr. (1985) Supp SCC 137

In this case, a petition was filed under Article 32 challenging the validity of Section 497 of IPC. The challenge was based on the fact that the said provision does not provide the right to a woman to prosecute the woman with whom her husband has committed adultery and hence is discriminatory. The 3 judge bench in this case also upheld the validity by stating that extending the ambit of offence should be done by the legislature and not by courts. The offence of breaking a family is no smaller than breaking a house, so the punishment is justified. The court accepted that only men can commit such an offence.

V. Revathi vs. Union of India (1988) 2 SCC 72

In this case, the court upheld the constitutional validity of Section 497 read with Section 198 by stating that this provision disables both wife and husband from punishing each other for adultery hence not discriminatory. It only punishes an outsider who tries to destroy the sanctity of marriage. And thus it is reverse discrimination in 'favour' of her rather than 'against' her.

W. Kalyani vs. State through Inspector of Police and another (2012) 1 SC 358

The constitutionality of Section 497 did not arise in this case but it says that mere fact that appellant is a woman makes her completely immune to the charge of adultery and she cannot be proceeded against for that offence.

RECOMENDATIONS :

1. In the 42nd Law Commission report, it was recommended to include adulterous women liable for prosecution and reduce punishment from 5 years to 2 years. It was not given effect.

2. In the 152nd Law Commission report, it was recommended introducing equality between sexes in the provision for adultery and reflecting the societal change with regards to the status of a woman. But it was not accepted.

3. In 2003, the Malimath Committee on Reforms of Criminal Justice System was formed which recommended amending the provision as 'whosoever has sexual intercourse with a spouse of any other is guilty of adultery'. The same is pending for consideration.

JUDGMENT :

Issue 1

The test of manifest arbitrariness should be applied to invalidate the legislation or any sub-legislation. Any law found arbitrary will be struck down.

Judgments cited:

E.P. Royappa vs. State of Tamil Nadu (1974) 4 SCC 3

ShayaraBano v. Union of India (2017) 9 SCC 1

1. The classification is found to be arbitrary in the sense that it treats only the husband as an aggrieved person given the right to prosecute for the offence and no such right is provided to the wife. The provision is not based on equality.

2. The offence is based on the notion of women being a property of husband and adultery is considered to be a theft of his property because it says consent or connivance by the husband would not make it an offence.

3. The provision does not treat the wife as an offender and punishes only the third party.

Such classification is arbitrary and discriminatory and has no relevance in present times where women have their own identity and stand equal to men in every aspect of life. This provision clearly violates Article 14.

Issue 2

1. This provision discriminates between a married man and a married woman to her detriment on the ground of sex.

2. This provision is based on the stereotype that a man has control over his wife's sexuality and she is his property. It perpetuates the notion that women are passive and incapable of exercising their sexual freedom.

3. Section 497 protects women from being punished as abettors. It is enunciated that this provision is beneficial for women, which is saved by Article 15(3). Article 15(3) was inserted to protect the women from patriarchy and pull them out of suppression. This article was aimed to bring them equal to men. But Section 497 is not protective discrimination but grounded in patriarchy and paternalism.

Judgments cited

Government of Andhra Pradesh v. P B Vijayakumar (1995) 4 SCC 520

Independent Thought vs. Union of India (2017) 10 SCC 800

Thus the said provision violates Article 15(1) of the constitution because it is discriminatory on the basis of gender and perpetuating the stereotype of controlling a wife's sexual autonomy.

Issue 3

The dignity of an individual and sexual privacy is protected by the constitution under Article 21. A woman has an equal right to privacy as a man. The autonomy of an individual is the ability to make decisions on vital matters of life.

Judgments cited

S. Puttaswamy and Anr. vs Union of India and others (2017) 10 SCC 1

Common Cause v. Union of India and ors. (2018) 5 SCC 1

1. The provision allows adultery on the husband's consent or connivance, which gives a man control over her sexual autonomy. This makes her a puppet of the husband and takes away all her individuality.

2. When the penal code was drafted the societal thinking regarding women was backward and she was treated as a chattel but after 158 years the status of women is equal to that of men. Her dignity is of utmost importance which cannot be undermined by a provision which perpetuates such gender stereotypes.

3. Treating women as victims also demeans her individuality and questions her identity without her husband.

The enforcement of forced fidelity by curtailing sexual autonomy is an affront to the fundamental right to dignity and equality provided under Article 21.

Issue 4

1. A crime is defined as an offence which affects society as a whole. Adultery, on the other hand, is an offence which tantamounts to entering into the private realm.

2. Adultery may be committed by two consenting adults making it a victimless crime.

3. This provision aims to protect the sanctity of marriage but we have to admit that because of a pre-existing disruption of marital tie adultery is committed.

4. The other offences related to matrimonial realms such as Section 306, 498-A, 304-B, 494 or any violation of Protection of women from Domestic Violence Act, 2005 or violation of Section 125 CrPC are related to the extinction of the life of a married woman and punishes her husband and relatives.

5. In adultery, a third party is punished for a criminal offence with a maximum 5 years imprisonment. This is not required in the opinion of the court.

6. This provision makes a husband an aggrieved person and a woman a victim. Even if the law changes and provides equal rights to women against adultery, it is totally a private matter.

7. Adultery is better left as a ground for divorce and not a crime.

Section 497 of IPC is struck down and adultery can be grounds for any civil wrong including dissolution of marriage.

## CRITICAL ANALYSIS :

Infidelity is more common in larger cities where people are moving towards westernization. This decision has been widely criticized on the ground that it paved a way for people to commit adultery without any fear. There has been an increase in adultery since its decriminalization. Males have claimed that now there is no way to ensure the purity of bloodline. Many claims that recommendations from Law Commissions should have been accepted by the parliament in order to punish men and women both equally for adultery. The Supreme Court has also been criticized that they should have let parliament take decisions on adultery according to the changing social environment. The Legislature should have taken this step long ago but nevertheless our judiciary has been very efficient in filling the gaps and removing redundant laws with changing societal notions.

CHAPTER TWELVE

# THE SUPREME COURT OF INDIA FOR PROPERTY RIGHT TO WOMEN

# A) VINEETA SHARMA VS RAKESH SHARMA (2020) 9 SCC 1

DECIDED ON : 11 August 2020

CASE NO. Civil Appeal No. : 32601 of 2018

BENCH : Arun Mishra, S. Abdul Nazeer, M.R. Shah J.J

There were three judges of the Supreme Court we are dealing with in this case in which they gave their judgment that the daughter gets right in the property from birth as a son. The father is dead or alive, it will not affect her right to the property. The verdict of Vineeta Sharma has cleared the uncertainty about the law & made it clear that the amendment of the Hindu Succession Act, granting equal right to inherit the ancestral property to daughters would have a retrospective effect. Court also perceived that gender cannot be the ground for denying anyone with their inheritance rights as it is a violation of Article 14 i.e. equality before law. This verdict has successfully resolved all the ambiguity that the Phulavati and Danamma case created.

CHAPTER THIRTEEN

# THE SUPREME COURT OF INDIA IN RIGHT TO EDUCATION

# A) MOHINI JAIN V. STATE OF KARNATAKA 1992 AIR 1858

The Court, in the absence of any Constitutional Provision for the Right to Education, held that the right to life and personal liberty under Article 21 includes the Right to Education as education is required for the overall development of personality, without which one would not be able to have the enjoyment of his right to life. The purpose of the right to life is baseless without the Right to Education.

## B) UNNI KRISHNAN, J.P & ORS. V. STATE OF ANDHRA PRADESH & ORS. 1993 AIR 217

By narrowing the approach taken by the Mohini Jain case, the Supreme Court held that the Right to Education is undoubtedly a Fundamental Right that stems from Article 21. However, the right to free education is available to children until they attain the age of 14 years; after that, the obligation of the state to provide education is subject to economic capacity and development.

# C) AVINASH MEHROTRA V. UNION OF INDIA 6 SCC 398 (2009)

The Court held that it is a fundamental right to have access to education free from the fear of security and shall have appropriate safety measures in case of any threat to life. Therefore, the right to education includes providing safe schools in accordance with Articles 21 and 21A of the Constitution. No matter where a family seeks to educate its children, even if it is a private institution, the state must ensure that children suffer no harm in exercising their fundamental right to education.

CHAPTER FOURTEEN

# THE SUPREME COURT OF INDIA FOR PROTCTION OF SOIL AND DRINKING WATER AND FOR SUSTAINABLE DEVELOPMENT

# Vellore Citizens Welfare Forum vs Union Of India & Ors on 28 August, 1996

(Looking on sustainable development, "precautionary principle" and the "polluter pays" principle was implemented.)

Bench: Kuldip Singh, Faizan Uddin, K. Venkataswami

FACTS OF THE CASE:

1. This petition - public interest – under Article 32 of the Constitution of India has been filed by Vellore Citizens Welfare Forum and is directed against the pollution which is being caused by enormous discharge of untreated effluent by the tanneries and other industries in the State of Tamil Nadu . It is stated that the tanneries are discharging untreated effluent into agricultural fields to, road-Sides, Water ways and open lands. The untreated effluent is finally discharged in river Palar which is the main source of water supply to the residents of the area.

2. According to the petitioner the entire surface and sub-soil water of river Palar has been polluted resulting in non availability Potable water to the residents of the area. It is stated that the tanneries in the State of Tamil Nadu have caused environmental degradation in the area. According to the preliminary survey made by the Tamil Nadu Agricultural University Research Center Vellore nearly 35,000 hectares of agricultural land in the Tanneries Belt, has become either partially or totally unfit for cultivation. It has been further stated in the petition that the tanneries use about 170 types of chemicals in the chrome tanning processes.

3. The said chemicals include sodium chloride, lime, sodium sulphate, chlorium sulphate, fat liquor Amonia and sulphuric acid besides dyes which are used in large quantities. Nearly 35 litres of water is used for processing one kilogram of finished leather, resulting in dangerously enormous quantities of toxic effluents being let out in the open by the tanning industry.

4. Thus these effluents have spoiled the physico-chemical properties of the soil, and have contaminated ground water by percolation.

JUDGMENT:

In the Government Order first read above, the Government have ordered, among other things, that no industry causing serious water pollution should be permitted with in one kilometer from the embankments of rivers, streams, dams etc, and that the Tamil Nadu Pollution Control Board Should furnish a list of such industries to all local bodies. It has been suggested that it is necessary to have a sharper definition for water sources so that ephemeral water collections like rein water ponds, drains, sewerages (bio-degradable) etc. may be excluded form the purview of the above order. The Chairman, Tamil Nadu Pollution Control Board has stated that the scope of the Government Order may be restricted to reservoirs, rivers and public drinking water sources.

He has also stated that there should be a complete ban on location of highly polluting industries within 1 Kilometer of certain water sources.

2. The Government have carefully examined the above suggestions. The Government impose a total ban on the setting up of the highly polluting industries mentioned in Annexure - I to this order ' within one Kilometer from the embankments of the water sources mentioned in Annexure-II to this order.

3. The Government direct that under any circumstance if any highly polluting industry is proposed to be set up within one kilometer from the embankments of water sources other than those mentioned in Annexure-II to this order, the Tamil Nadu Pollution Control Board should examine the case and obtain the approval of the Government for it".

Annexure-I to the Notification includes Distilleries, tanneries, fertilizer, steel plants and foundries as the highly polluting industries. We have our doubts whether the above quoted government order is being enforced by the Tamil Nadu Government. The order has been issued to control pollution and protect the environment. We are of the view that the order should be strictly enforced and no industry listed in Annexure-l to the order should be permitted to be set up in the prohibited area.

Learned counsel for the tanneries raised an objection that the standard regarding total dissolved solids (TDS) fixed by the Board was no. justified. This Court by the order date April 9, 1996 directed the NEERI to examine this aspect and give its opinion. In its report dated June 11, 1996 NEERI has justified the standards stipulated by the Board. The reasoning of the NEERI given in its report dated June 11, 1996 is as under:

"The total dissolved solids in ambient water have phisiological, industrial and economic significance. The consumer acceptance of mineralized water decreases in direct proportion to increased mineralization as indicated by Bruvold (1). High Total dissolved solids (TDS), including chlorides and sulphates, are objectionable due to possible physiological effect and mineral taste that they impart to water. High levels of total dissolved solids produce Laxative/cathartic/purgative effect in consumers. the requirement of soap and other detergents in household and industry is directly related to water hardness as brought out by DeBoer and Larsen (2). High concentration of mineral salts, particularly sulphates and chlorides, are also associated with costly corrosion damage in wastewater treatment systems, as detailed by patterson and Banker (3). Of par particular importance is the tendency of scale deposits with high TDS thereby resulting in high fuel consumption in boilers. The Ministry of Environment and forests (MEF) has not categorically laid down standards for inland surface water discharge for total dissolved solids (TDS), sulphates and chlorides. The Decision on these standards rests with the respective state Pollution Control Boards as per the requirements based on local site conditions. The standards stipulated by the TNPCB are justified on the aforereffered considerations.

The prescribed standards of the TNPCB for inland surfaces water discharge can be met for tannery wastewaters cost-effectively through proper implant control measures in tanning operation, and rationally designed and effectively operated wastewater treatment plants (ETPs & CETPs). Tables 3 and 5 depict the quality of groundwater in some areas around tanneries during peak summer period (June 3- 5, 1996). Table 8 presents the data collection by TNPCB at individual ETPs indicating that TDS, sulphates and chlorides concentrations are below the prescribed standards for inland surface water discharge. The quality of ambient waters needs to the maintained through the standards stipulated by TNPCB."

The Board has Power under the Environment Act and the Rules to lay down standards for emissions or discharge of environmental Pollutants. Rule 3(2) of the Rules even permit the Board to specify more stringent standards from those provided under the Rules. The NEERI having justified the standards stipulated by the Board, We direct that these standards are to be maintained by the tanneries and other industries in the State of Tamil Nadu.

DIRECTIONS OF COURT:

1. The Central Government shall constitute an authority under Section 3(3) of the Environment (Protection) Act, 1986 and shall confer on the said authority all the powers necessary to deal with the situation created by the tanneries and other polluting industries in the State of Tamil Nadu. The Authority shall be headed by a retired judge of the High Court and it may have other members- preferably with expertise in the field of pollution control and environment protection- to be appointed by the Central Government. The Central Government shall confer on the said authority the powers to issue directions under Setion 5 of the Environment Act and for taking measures with respect to the matters referred to in Clause (v), (vi) (vii) (viii) (ix) (x) and (xii) of Sub-Section (2) of Setion 3. The Central Government shall consitute the authority before September 30, 1996.

2. The authority so constituted by the Central Government shall implement the "precautionary principle" and the "polluter pays" principle. The authority shall, with the help of expert opinion and after giving opportunity to the concerned polluters assess the loss to the ecology\ environment in the affected areas and shall also identify the individuals/ families who have suffered because of the pollution and shall assess the

compensation to be paid to the said individuals/families. The authority shall further determine the compensation to be recovered from the polluters as cost of reversing the damaged environment. The authority shall lay down just and fair procedure for completing the exercise.

3. The authority shall compute the compensation under two heads namely, for reversing the ecology and for payment to individuals. A statement showing the total amount to be recovered, the names of the polluters from who the amount is to be recovered, the amount to be recovered from each polluter, the persons to who the compensation is to be paid and the amount payable to each of them shall be forwarded to the Collector\District Magistrates of the area concerned. The Collector\ District magistrate shall recover the amount from the polluters, if necessary, as arrears of land revenue. He shall disburse the compensation awarded by the authority to be affected persons/families.

4. The authority shall direct the closure of the industry owned/managed by a polluter in case he evades or refuses to pay the compensation awarded against him. This shall be in addition to the recovery from his as arrears of land revenue.

5. An industry may have set up the necessary pollution control device at present but it shall be liable to pay for the past pollution generated by the said industry which has resulted in the environmental degradation and suffering to the residents of the area.

6. We impose pollution fine of Rs. 10,000/- each on all the tanneries in the districts of North Arcot Ambedkar, Erode Periyar, Dindigul Anna, Trichi and Chengai M.G.R. The fine shall be paid before October 31, 1996 in the office of the Collector/District Magistrate concerned. We direct the Collectors/District Magistrates of these districts to recover the fines from the tanneries. The money shall be deposited, alongwith the compensation amount recovered from the polluters, under a separate head called "Environment protection Fund" and shall be utilised for compensating the affected persons as identified by the authorities and also for restoring the damaged environment. The pollution fine is liable to the recovered as arrears of land revenue. The tanneries which fail to deposit the amount by

October 31, 1996 shall be closed forthwith and shall also be liable under the Contempt of Court Act.

7. The authority, in consultation with expert bodies like NEERI, Central Board, Board shall frame scheme/schemes for reversing the damage caused to the ecology and environment by pollution in the State of Tamil Nadu. The scheme/schemes so framed shall be executed by the State Government under the supervision of the Central Government. The expenditure shall be met from the "Environment protection fund" and from other sources provided by the state Government and the Central Government.

8. We suspend the closure orders in respect of all the tanneries in the five districts of North Arcot Ambedkar, Erode Periyar, Dindigul Anna, Trichi and Chengai M.G.R. We direct all the tanneries in the above five districts to set up CETPs or Individual Pollution control Devices on or before November 30, 1996. Those connected with CETPs shall have to install in addition the primary devices in the tanerries. All the tanneries in the above five districts shall obtain the consent of the Board to function and operate with effect from December 15, 1996. The tanneries who are refused consent or who fail to obtain the consent of the Board by December 15, 1996 shall be closed forthwith.

9. We direct the Superintendent of Police and the Collector/district Magistrate/Deputy Commissioner of the district concerned to close all those tanneries with immediate effect who fail to obtain the consent from the Board by the said date. Such tanneries shall not be reopened unless the authority permits them to do so. It would be open to the authority to close such tanneries permanently or to direct their relocation.

10. The Government Order No. 213 dated March 30, 1989 shall be enforced forthwith. No. new industry listed in Annexure-I to the Notification shall be permitted to be set up within the prohibited area. The authority shall review the case of all the industries which are already operating in the prohibited area and it would be open to authority to direct the relocation of any of such industries.

11. The standards stipuated by the Board regarding total dissolved solids (TDS) and approved by the NEERI shall be operative. All the tanneries and other industries in the State of Tamil Nadu shall comply with the said standards. The quality of ambient waters has to be maintained through the standards stipulated by the Board.

We have issued comprehensive directions for achieving the end result in this case. It is not necesary for this Court to monitor these matters any further. we are of the view that the Madras High Court would be in a better position to monitor these matters hereinafter. We, therefore, request the Chief Justice of the Madras High Court to constitute a special Bench "Green bench" to deal with this case and other environmental matters. We make it clear that it would be open to the Bench to pass any appropriate order/orders keeping in view the directions issued by us. We may mention that "Green Benches" are already functioning in Calcutta, Madhya Pradesh and some other High Courts. We Direct the Registry of this Court to send the records to the registry of the Madras High matter as a petition under Article 226 of the Constitution of India and deal with it in accordance with law and also in terms of the directions issued by us. We give liberty to the parties to approach the High Court as and when necessary.

Mr. M.C. Mehta has been assisting this Court to our utmost satisfaction. We place on record our appreciation for Mr. Mehta. We direct the State of Tamil Nadu to pay Rs. 50,000/- towards legal fees and other out of pocket expenses incurred by Mr. Mehta.

CHAPTER FIFTEEN

# THE SUPREME COURT OF INDIA FOR PROTCTION OF BASIC HUMAN RIGHTS

# A)Shri D.K. Basu,Ashok K. Johri vs State Of West Bengal,State Of U.P on 18 December, 1996

(Due to custodial violence and deaths in police lock up, court has formulated certain guideline for police to check atrocities on accused / victim and compensation was also awarded by

Author: A. S. Anand

Bench: Kuldip Singh, A.S. Anan

FACT OF THE CASE:-

The Executive Chairman, Legal Aid Services, West Bengal, a non-political organisation registered under the Society Registration Act, on 26th August, 1986 addressed a letter to the Chief Justice of India drawing his attention to certain news items published in the Telegraph dated 20, 21 and 22 of July, 1986 and in the Statesman and Indian express dated 17th August, 1986 regarding deaths in police lock-ups and custody.

The Executive Chairman after reproducing the new items submitted that it was imperative to examine the issue in depth and to develop "custody jurisprudence" and formulate modalities for awarding compensation to the victim and /or family members of the victim for attrocities and death caused in police custody and to provide for accountability of the efforts are often made to hush up the matter of lock-up deaths and thus the crime goes unpunished and "flourishes". It was requested that the letter alongwith the new items be treated as a writ petition under "public interest litigation" category.

Considering the importance of the issue raised in the letter being concerned by frequent complaints regarding custodial violence and deaths in police lock up, the letter was treated as a writ petition and notice was issued on 9.2.1987 to the respondents.

In response to the notice, the State of West Bengal filed a counter. It was maintained that the police was no hushing up any matter of lock-up death and that where ever police personnel were found to be responsible for such death, action was being initiated against them. The respondents characterised the writ petition as misconceived, misleading and untenable in law.

While the writ petition was under consideration a letter addressed by Shri Ashok Kumar Johri on 29.7.87 to the Hon'ble Chief Justice of India drawing the attention of this Court to the death of one Mahesh Bihari of Pilkhana, Aligarh in police custody was received. That letter was also treated as a writ petition and was directed to be listed alongwith the writ petition filed by Shri D.K. Basu. On 14.8.1987 this Court made the following order :

Mr. D. K. Basu was one of the Petitioners in this case. He was Judge of Calcutta High Court and the Chairman of Legal Aid Services West Bengal (LASWEB). DK Basu, Executive Chairman of Legal Aid Services, West Bengal, a non-political organization on 26/08/1986 addressed a letter to the Supreme Court of India calling his attention to certain news published in the Telegraph Newspaper about deaths in police custody and custody. He requested that the letter be treated as a Writ Petition within the "Public Interest Litigation". Considering the importance of the issues raised in the letter, it was treated as a written Petition and the Defendants were notified.

JUDGMENT:

"Custodial torture" is a naked violation of human dignity and degradation with destroys, to a very large extent, the individual personality. IT is a calculated assault on human dignity and whenever human dignity is wounded, civilisation takes a step backward-flag of humanity must on each such occasion fly half-mast.

In all custodial crimes that is of real concern is not only infliction of body pain but the mental agony which a person undergoes within the four walls of police station or lock-up. Whether it is physical assault or rape in police custody, the extent of trauma a person experiences is beyond the purview of law.

"Custodial violence" and abuse of police power is not only peculiar to this country, but it is widespread. It has been the concern of international community because the problem is universal and the challenge is almost global. The Universal Declaration of Human Rights in 1984, which market the emergency of worldwide trend of protection and guarantee of certain basic human rights, stipulates in Article 5 that "No one shall be subjected to torture or to curel, inhuman or degrading treatment or punishment." Despite the pious declaration, the crime continues unabated, though every civilised nation shows its concern and takes steps for its eradication.

It was considering these aspects that the Law Commission in its 113th Report recommended the insertion of Section 114B in the Indian Evidence Act. The Law Commission recommended in its 113th Report that in prosecution of a police officer for an alleged offence of having caused bodily injury to a person, if there was evidence that the injury was caused during the period when the person was in the custody of the police, the Court may presume that the injury was caused by the police officer having the custody of the person during that period. The Commission further recommended that the court, while considering the question of presumption, should have regard to all relevant circumstances including the period of custody statement made by the victim, medical evidence and the evidence with the Magistrate may have recorded. Change of burden of proof was, thus, advocated.

Police is, no doubt, under a legal duty and has legitimate right to arrest a criminal and to interrogate him during the investigation of a an offence but it must be remembered that the law does not permit use of third degree methods or torture of accused in custody during interrogation and investigation with that view to solve the crime. End cannot justify the means. The interrogation and investigation into a crime should be in true sense purpose full to make the investigation effective. By torturing a person and using their degree methods, the police would be accomplishing behind the closed doors what the demands of our legal order forbid. No. society can permit it.

How do we check the abuse of police power? Transparency of action and accountability perhaps are tow possible safeguards which this Court must insist upon. Attention is also required to be paid to properly develop work culture, training and orientation of police force consistent with basic human values. Training methodology of the police needs restructuring. The force needs to be infused with basic human values and made sensitive to the constitutional ethos. Efforts must be made to change the attitude and approach of the police personal handling investigations so that they do not sacrifice basic human values during interrogation and do not resort to questionable form of interrogation. With a view to bring in transparency, the presence of the counsel of the arrestee at some point of time during the interrogation may deter the police from using third degree methods during interrogation.

Apart from the police, there are several other governmental authorities also like Directorate of Revenue Intelligence, Directorate of Enforcement, Costal Guard, Central Reserve Police Force (CRPF), Border Security Force (BSF), the Central Industrial Security Force (CISF), the State Armed Police, Intelligence Agencies like the Intelligence Bureau, R.A.W, Central Bureau of Investigation (CBI) , CID, Tariff Police, Mounted Police and ITBP which have the power to detain a person and to interrogated him in connection with the investigation of economic offences, offences under the Essential Commodities Act, Excise and Customs Act. Foreign Exchange Regulation Act etc. There are instances of torture and death in custody of these authorities as well, In re Death of Sawinder Singh Grover [1995 Supp (4) SCC, 450], (to which Kuldip Singh, j. was a party) this Court took suo moto notice of the death of Sawinder Singh Grover during his custody with the Directorate of Enforcement. After getting an enquiry conducted by the additional District Judge, which disclosed a prima facie case for investigation and prosecution, this Court directed the CBI to lodge a FIR and initiate criminal proceeding against all persons named in the report of the Additional District Judge and proceed against them. The Union of India/Directorate of Enforcement was also directed to pay sum of Rs. 2 lacs to the widow of the deceased by was of the relevant provisions of law to protect the interest of arrested persons in such cases too is a genuine need.

There is one other aspect also which needs out consideration, We are conscious of the fact that the police in India have to perform a difficult and delicate task, particularly in view of the deteriorating law and order situation, communal riots, political turmoil, student unrest, terrorist activities, and among others the increasing number of underworld and armed gangs and criminals, Many hard core criminals like extremist, the terrorists, drug peddlers, smugglers who have organised gangs, have taken strong roots in the society. It is being said in certain quarters that with more and more liberalisation and enforcement of fundamental rights, it would lead to difficulties in the detection of crimes committed by such categories of hardened criminals by soft peddling interrogation. It is felt in those quarters that if we lay to much of emphasis on protection of their fundamental rights and human rights such criminals may go scot-free without exposing any element or iota or criminality with the result, the crime would go unpunished and in the ultimate analysis the society would suffer. The concern is genuine and the problem is real. To deal with such a situation, a balanced approach is needed to meet the ends of justice. This all the more so, in view of the expectation of the society that police must deal with the criminals in an efficient and effective manner and bring to book those who are involved in the crime. The cure cannot, however, be worst than the disease itself.

In addition to the statutory and constitutional requirements to which we have made a reference, we are of the view that it would be useful and effective to structure appropriate machinery for contemporaneous recording and notification of all cases of arrest and detention to bring in transparency and accountability. It is desirable that the officer arresting a person should prepare a memo of his arrest on witness who may be a member of the family of the arrestee or a respectable person of the locality from where the arrest is made. The date and time of arrest shall be recorded in The memo which must also be counter signed by The arrestee.

We therefore, consider it appropriate to issue the following requirements to be followed in all cases of arrest or detention till legal provisions are made in that behalf as preventive measures :

(1) The police personnel carrying out the arrest and handling the interrogation of the arrestee should bear accurate, visible and clear identification and name togs with their designations. The particulars of all such police personnel who handle interrogation of the arrestee must be recorded in a register.

(2) That the police officer carrying out the arrest of the arrestee shall prepare a memo of arrest at the time of arrest a such memo shall be attested by atleast one witness. who may be either a member of the family of the arrestee or a respectable person of the locality from where the arrest is made. It shall also be counter signed by the arrestee and shall contain the time and date of arrest. (3) A person who has been arrested or detained and is being held in custody in a police station or interrogation centre or other lock-up, shall be entitled to have one friend or relative or other person known to him or having interest in his welfare being informed, as soon as practicable, that he has been arrested and is being detained at the particular place, unless the attesting witness of the memo of arrest is himself such a friend or a relative of the arrestee. (4) The time, place of arrest and venue of custody of an arrestee must be notified by the police where the next friend or relative of the arrestee lives outside the district or town through the legal Aid Organisation in the District and the police station of the area concerned telegraphically within a period of 8 to 12 hours after the arrest.

(5) The person arrested must be made aware of this right to have someone informed of his arrest or detention as soon he is put under arrest or is detained.

(6) An entry must be made in the diary at the place of detention regarding the arrest of the person which shall also disclose the name of he next friend of the person who has been informed of the arrest an the names

and particulars of the police officials in whose custody the arrestee is. (7) The arrestee should, where he so requests, be also examined at the time of his arrest and major and minor injuries, if any present on his/her body, must be recorded at that time. The "Inspection Memo" must be signed both by the arrestee and the police officer effecting the arrest and its copy provided to the arrestee.

(8) The arrestee should be subjected to medical examination by trained doctor every 48 hours during his detention in custody by a doctor on the panel of approved doctors appointed by Director, Health Services of the concerned Stare or Union Territory. Director, Health Services should prepare such a penal for all Tehsils and Districts as well. (9) Copies of all the documents including the memo of arrest, referred to above, should be sent to the illaga Magistrate for his record.

(10) The arrestee may be permitted to meet his lawyer during interrogation, though not throughout the interrogation.

(11) A police control room should be provided at all district and state headquarters, where information regarding the arrest and the place of custody of the arrestee shall be communicated by the officer causing the arrest, within 12 hours of effecting the arrest and at the police control room it should be displayed on a conspicuous notice board.

Failure to comply with the requirements hereinabove mentioned shall apart from rendering the concerned official liable for departmental action, also render his liable to be punished for contempt of court and the proceedings for contempt of court may be instituted in any High Court of the country, having territorial jurisdiction over the matter.

The requirements, referred to above flow from Articles 21 and 22 (1) of the Constitution and need to be strictly followed. These would apply with equal force to the other governmental agencies also to which a reference has been made earlier.

These requirements are in addition to the constitutional and statutory safeguards and do not detract from various other directions given by the courts from time to time in connection with the safeguarding of the rights and dignity of the arrestee.

The requirements mentioned above shall be forwarded to the Director General of Police and the Home Secretary of every Stare/Union Territory and it shall be their obligation to circulate the same to every police station under their charge and get the same notified at every police station at conspicuous place. It would also be useful and serve larger interest to broadcast the requirements on the All India Radio besides being shown on the National network of Doordarshan and by publishing and distributing pamphlets in the local language containing these requirements for information of the general public. Creating awareness about the rights of the arrestee would in out opinion be a step in the right direction to combat the evil of custodial crime and bring in transparency and accountability. It is hoped that these requirements would help to curb, if not totally eliminate, the use of questionable methods during interrogation and investigation leading to custodial commission of crimes.

PUNITIVE MEASURES UBI JUS IBI REMEDIUM - There is no wrong without a remedy. The law will that in every case where man is wronged and undamaged he must have a remedy. A mere declaration of invalidity of an action or finding of custodial violence or death in lock-up does not by itself provide any meaningful remedy to a person whose fundamental right to life has been infringed. Much more needs to be done.

A similar approach of redressing the wrong by award of monetary compensation against the State for its failure to protect the fundamental rights of the citizen has been adopted by the Courts of Ireland, which has a written constitution, guaranteeing fundamental rights, but which also like the Indian Constitution contains no provision of remedy for the infringement of those rights. That has, however, not prevented the Court in Ireland from developing remedies, including the award of damages, not only against individuals guilty of infringement, but against the State itself.

Thus, to sum up, it is now a well accepted proposition in most of the jurisdictions, that monetary or pecuniary compensation is an appropriate and indeed an effective and sometimes perhaps the only suitable remedy for redressal of the established infringement of the fundamental right to life of a citizen by the public servants and the State is vicariously liable for their acts. The claim of the citizen is based on the principle of strict liability to which the defence of sovereign immunity is not available and the citizen must revive the amount of compensation from the State, which shall have the right to be indemnified by the wrong doer. In the assessment of compensation, the emphasis has to be on the compensatory and not on punitive element. The objective is to apply balm to the wounds and not to punish the transgressor or the offender, as awarding appropriate punishment for the offender, as awarding appropriate punishment for the offence (irrespective of compensation) must be left to the criminal courts in which the offender is prosecuted, which the State, in law, is duty bound to do, That award of compensation in the public law jurisdiction is also without prejudice to any other action like civil suit for damages which is lawfully available to the victim or the heirs of the deceased victim with respect to the same matter for the tortious act committed by the functionaries of the State. The quantum of compensation will of course, depend upon the peculiar facts of each case and no strait jacket formula can be evolved in that behalf. The relief to redress the wrong for the established invasion of the fundamental rights of the citizen, under the public law jurisdiction is, in addition to the traditional remedies and not it derrogation of them. The amount of compensation as awarded by the Court and paid by the State to redress the wrong done, may in a given case, be adjusted against any amount which may be awarded to the claimant by way of damages in a civil suit.

## B) Vishakha and others v State of Rajasthan

(In 1997, the Supreme Court laid down guidelines in the Vishaka case, pending formal legislation, for dealing with sexual harassment of women at the workplace. Later on The Sexual Harassment of Women at Workplace (Prevention, Prohibition and Redressal) Act, 2013 ("Sexual Harassment Act") has been made effective on April 23, 2013 by way of publication in the Gazette of India.)

FACTS OF THE CASE:

Vishakha and others v State of Rajasthan was a 1997 Indian Supreme Court case where Vishakha and other women groups filed Public Interest Litigation (PIL) against State of Rajasthan and Union of India to enforce the fundamental rights of working women under Articles 14, 19 and 21 of the Constitution of India.

The petition was filed after Bhanwari Devi, a social worker in Rajasthan was brutally gang raped for stopping a child marriage.[1] The court decided that the consideration of "International Conventions and norms are significant for the purpose of interpretation of the guarantee of gender equality, right to work with human dignity in Articles 14, 15 19(1)(g) and 21 of the Constitution and the safeguards againstsexual harassment implicit therein."

The petition, resulted in what are popularly known as the Vishaka Guidelines. The judgment of August 1997 given by a bench of J. S. Verma (then C.J.I)., Sujata Manohar and B. N. Kirpal, provided the basic definitions of sexual harassment at the workplace and provided guidelines to deal with it. It is seen as a significant legal victory for women's groups in India.[1][2][3]

In India before 1997, There was no formal guidelines for how an incident involving sexual harassment at workplace should be dealt by an employer. Women experiencing sexual harassment at workplace had to lodge a complaint under Section 354 of the Indian Penal Code that deals with the 'criminal assault of women to outrage women's modesty', and Section 509 that punishes an individual or individuals for using a ‘word, gesture or act intended to insult the modesty of a woman’. These sections left the interpretation of ‘outraging women’s modesty’ to the discretion of the police officer.

The court decided that the consideration of "International Conventions and norms are significant for the purpose of interpretation of the guarantee of gender equality, right to work with human dignity in Articles 14, 15 19(1)(g) and 21 of the Constitution and the safeguards against sexual harassment implicit therein." Supreme Court of India defined sexual harassment and set guidelines for employers.

What is sexual harassment

Sexual harassment includes such unwelcome sexually determined behaviour (whether directly or by implication) as:

a) physical contact and advances;

b) a demand or request for sexual favours;

c) sexually coloured remarks;

d) showing pornography;

e) any other unwelcome physical verbal or non-verbal conduct of sexual nature.

Where any of these acts is committed in circumstances where under the victim of such conduct has a reasonable apprehension that in relation to the victim’s employment or work whether she is drawing salary, or honorarium or voluntary, whether in government, public or private enterprise such conduct can be humiliating and may constitute a health and safety problem.

It is discriminatory for instance when the woman has reasonable grounds to believe that her objection would disadvantage her in connection with her employment or work including recruiting or promotion or when it creates a hostile work environment. Thus, sexual harassment need NOT involve physical contact. Any act that creates a hostile work environment - be it by virtue of cracking lewd jokes, verbal abuse, circulating lewd rumours etc. counts as sexual harassment.[6]

The creation of a hostile work environment through unwelcome physical verbal or non-verbal conduct of sexual nature may consist not of a single act but of pattern of behaviour comprising many such acts.

Thus, it is important that the victim report such behaviour as soon as possible and not wait for it to become worse. In some cases, the psychological stigma of reporting the conduct of a co-worker might require a great deal of courage on the part of the victim and they may report such acts after a long period of time. The guidelines suggest that the complaint mechanism should ensure time bound treatment of complaints, but they do not suggest that a report can only be made within a short period of time since the incident occurred.

Often, the police refuse to lodge FIRs for sexual harassment cases, especially where the harassment occurred some time ago.[7]

## From guidelines to Act

The Supreme Court of India's judgement only proposed guidelines to alleviate the problem of sexual harassment in 1997. India finally enacted its law on prevention of sexual harassment against female employees at the workplace. The Sexual Harassment of Women at Workplace (Prevention, Prohibition and Redressal) Act, 2013 ("Sexual Harassment Act") has been made effective on April 23, 2013 by way of publication in the Gazette of India.[8]

CHAPTER SIXTEEN

# CONCLUSIONS

In this way we see that the law has great impact on the development of rural infrastructure and for the development of rural people. The law not only provides rural people for their economic development but it also strengthen them politically by providing Panchayati Raj by the amendments in the constitution. It also provides rural people justice to their doorsteps by the help of Gram Nayayalay and through the legal service authority. They have also got access of information through Right to Information Act with the help of information technology even sitting in their own house. It also provides fair compensation to the people of rural area when their land is acquired by the government for any specific work.

We have also seen that the law of this nation provided women equal rights on her father`s property like son / male person. On the basis of law of our country Supreme Court have passed so many judgments which eradicate the evils of our society, like, in the case of Shakti Vahini v Union of India, the court laid down guidelines that need to be implemented by the government for the eradication of Honour killing in India. Court also tried to protect our environment in Vellore Citizens Welfare Forum vs Union of India & Ors case and Looking on sustainable development, "precautionary principle" and the "polluter pays" principle was implemented and protected interest of the rural people.

In this way we see that the law plays a very vital role in the development of people of village area in many ways. Because the development of village is the development of our nation, as majority of people live there.

# References

ACTS:

Prohibition of Sati Act 1829, Sti Abolition Act

The Child Marriage Restraint Act, 1929

The Prohibition of Child Marriage Act, 2006

Prohibition of Child Marriage (Amendment) Bill 2021

Hindu Marriage Act of 1955

Gram Nyayalayas Act, 2008

Right to Education (RTE) Act 2009

73rd Constitutional Amendment Act 1992

The Cigarettes and Other tobacco products (prohibition of advertisement and regulation of trade and commerce, production, supply and distribution) act, 2003 no. 34 of 2003

Public Health Act 2007

Mahatma Gandhi National Rural Employment Guarantee Act, 2005 No. 42 OF 2005, (MGNREGA)

The Hindu succession amendment Act 2005

The National Highways Act, 1956

The Carriage by Road Act,

The Stage-Carriages Act, 1861

The Central Road and Infrastructure Fund Act, 2000

The Control of National Highways (land and traffic) Act, 2002

The Information Technology ACT, 2008

The Right to Information Act, 2005

Muslim Personal law (Shariat) Application Act 1937

JUDGMENTS OF THE COURT:

Shakti Vahini vs. Union of India & Ors. [2018] 3 SCR 770 : (2018) 7 SCC 192

Citation: WRIT PETITION (CIVIL) NO. 231 OF 2010

Vineeta Sharma Vs Rakesh Sharma (2020) 9 SCC 1DECIDED ON : 11 August 2020

Judgment on triple talak - Shayara Bano v. Union of India & Others, Writ Petition (C) No. 118 of 2016

Mohini Jain v. State of Karnataka 1992 AIR 1858

Unni Krishnan, J.P & Ors. v. State of Andhra Pradesh & Ors. 1993 AIR 217

Avinash Mehrotra v. Union of India 6 SCC 398 (2009)

Vellore Citizens Welfare Forum vs Union Of India & Ors on 28 August, 1996, AIR 1996 SC 2715: (1996) 5 SCC 647

ACTS:

Prohibition of Sati Act 1829, Sti Abolition Act

The Child Marriage Restraint Act, 1929

The Prohibition of Child Marriage Act, 2006

Prohibition of Child Marriage (Amendment) Bill 2021

Hindu Marriage Act of 1955

Gram Nyayalayas Act, 2008

Right to Education (RTE) Act 2009

73rd Constitutional Amendment Act 1992

The Cigarettes and Other tobacco products (prohibition of advertisement and regulation of trade and commerce, production, supply and distribution) act, 2003 no. 34 of 2003

Public Health Act 2007

Mahatma Gandhi National Rural Employment Guarantee Act, 2005 No. 42 OF 2005, (MGNREGA)

The Hindu succession amendment Act 2005

The National Highways Act, 1956

The Carriage by Road Act,

The Stage-Carriages Act, 1861

The Central Road and Infrastructure Fund Act, 2000

The Control of National Highways (land and traffic) Act, 2002

The Information Technology ACT, 2008

The Right to Information Act, 2005

Muslim Personal law (Shariat) Application Act 1937

JUDGMENTS OF THE COURT:

Shakti Vahini vs. Union of India & Ors. [2018] 3 SCR 770 : (2018) 7 SCC 192

Citation: WRIT PETITION (CIVIL) NO. 231 OF 2010

Vineeta Sharma Vs Rakesh Sharma (2020) 9 SCC 1DECIDED ON : 11 August 2020

Judgment on triple talak - Shayara Bano v. Union of India & Others, Writ Petition (C) No. 118 of 2016

Mohini Jain v. State of Karnataka 1992 AIR 1858

Unni Krishnan, J.P & Ors. v. State of Andhra Pradesh & Ors. 1993 AIR 217

Avinash Mehrotra v. Union of India 6 SCC 398 (2009)

Vellore Citizens Welfare Forum vs Union Of India & Ors on 28 August, 1996, AIR 1996 SC 2715: (1996) 5 SCC 647

ACTS:

Prohibition of Sati Act 1829, Sti Abolition Act

The Child Marriage Restraint Act, 1929

The Prohibition of Child Marriage Act, 2006

Prohibition of Child Marriage (Amendment) Bill 2021

Hindu Marriage Act of 1955

Gram Nyayalayas Act, 2008

Right to Education (RTE) Act 2009

73rd Constitutional Amendment Act 1992

The Cigarettes and Other tobacco products (prohibition of advertisement and regulation of trade and commerce, production, supply and distribution) act, 2003 no. 34 of 2003

Public Health Act 2007

Mahatma Gandhi National Rural Employment Guarantee Act, 2005 No. 42 OF 2005, (MGNREGA)

The Hindu succession amendment Act 2005

The National Highways Act, 1956

The Carriage by Road Act,

The Stage-Carriages Act, 1861

The Central Road and Infrastructure Fund Act, 2000

The Control of National Highways (land and traffic) Act, 2002

The Information Technology ACT, 2008

The Right to Information Act, 2005

Muslim Personal law (Shariat) Application Act 1937

JUDGMENTS OF THE COURT:

Shakti Vahini vs. Union of India & Ors. [2018] 3 SCR 770 : (2018) 7 SCC 192

Citation: WRIT PETITION (CIVIL) NO. 231 OF 2010

Vineeta Sharma Vs Rakesh Sharma (2020) 9 SCC 1DECIDED ON : 11 August 2020

Judgment on triple talak - Shayara Bano v. Union of India & Others, Writ Petition (C) No. 118 of 2016

Mohini Jain v. State of Karnataka 1992 AIR 1858

Unni Krishnan, J.P & Ors. v. State of Andhra Pradesh & Ors. 1993 AIR 217

Avinash Mehrotra v. Union of India 6 SCC 398 (2009)

Vellore Citizens Welfare Forum vs Union Of India & Ors on 28 August, 1996, AIR 1996 SC 2715: (1996) 5 SCC 647

ACTS:

Prohibition of Sati Act 1829, Sti Abolition Act

The Child Marriage Restraint Act, 1929

The Prohibition of Child Marriage Act, 2006

Prohibition of Child Marriage (Amendment) Bill 2021

Hindu Marriage Act of 1955

Gram Nyayalayas Act, 2008

Right to Education (RTE) Act 2009

73rd Constitutional Amendment Act 1992

The Cigarettes and Other tobacco products (prohibition of advertisement and regulation of trade and commerce, production, supply and distribution) act, 2003 no. 34 of 2003

Public Health Act 2007

Mahatma Gandhi National Rural Employment Guarantee Act, 2005 No. 42 OF 2005, (MGNREGA)

The Hindu succession amendment Act 2005

The National Highways Act, 1956

The Carriage by Road Act,

The Stage-Carriages Act, 1861

The Central Road and Infrastructure Fund Act, 2000

The Control of National Highways (land and traffic) Act, 2002

The Information Technology ACT, 2008

The Right to Information Act, 2005

Muslim Personal law (Shariat) Application Act 1937

JUDGMENTS OF THE COURT:

Shakti Vahini vs. Union of India & Ors. [2018] 3 SCR 770 : (2018) 7 SCC 192

Citation: WRIT PETITION (CIVIL) NO. 231 OF 2010

Vineeta Sharma Vs Rakesh Sharma (2020) 9 SCC 1DECIDED ON : 11 August 2020

Judgment on triple talak - Shayara Bano v. Union of India & Others, Writ Petition (C) No. 118 of 2016

Mohini Jain v. State of Karnataka 1992 AIR 1858

Unni Krishnan, J.P & Ors. v. State of Andhra Pradesh & Ors. 1993 AIR 217

Avinash Mehrotra v. Union of India 6 SCC 398 (2009)

Vellore Citizens Welfare Forum vs Union Of India & Ors on 28 August, 1996, AIR 1996 SC 2715: (1996) 5 SCC 647

ACTS:

Prohibition of Sati Act 1829, Sti Abolition Act

The Child Marriage Restraint Act, 1929

The Prohibition of Child Marriage Act, 2006

Prohibition of Child Marriage (Amendment) Bill 2021

Hindu Marriage Act of 1955

Gram Nyayalayas Act, 2008

Right to Education (RTE) Act 2009

73rd Constitutional Amendment Act 1992

The Cigarettes and Other tobacco products (prohibition of advertisement and regulation of trade and commerce, production, supply and distribution) act, 2003 no. 34 of 2003

Public Health Act 2007

Mahatma Gandhi National Rural Employment Guarantee Act, 2005 No. 42 OF 2005, (MGNREGA)

The Hindu succession amendment Act 2005

The National Highways Act, 1956

The Carriage by Road Act,

The Stage-Carriages Act, 1861

The Central Road and Infrastructure Fund Act, 2000

The Control of National Highways (land and traffic) Act, 2002

The Information Technology ACT, 2008

The Right to Information Act, 2005

Muslim Personal law (Shariat) Application Act 1937

JUDGMENTS OF THE COURT:

Shakti Vahini vs. Union of India & Ors. [2018] 3 SCR 770 : (2018) 7 SCC 192

Citation: WRIT PETITION (CIVIL) NO. 231 OF 2010

Vineeta Sharma Vs Rakesh Sharma (2020) 9 SCC 1DECIDED ON : 11 August 2020

Judgment on triple talak - Shayara Bano v. Union of India & Others, Writ Petition (C) No. 118 of 2016

Mohini Jain v. State of Karnataka 1992 AIR 1858

Unni Krishnan, J.P & Ors. v. State of Andhra Pradesh & Ors. 1993 AIR 217

Avinash Mehrotra v. Union of India 6 SCC 398 (2009)

Vellore Citizens Welfare Forum vs Union Of India & Ors on 28 August, 1996, AIR 1996 SC 2715: (1996) 5 SCC 647

ACTS:

Prohibition of Sati Act 1829, Sti Abolition Act

The Child Marriage Restraint Act, 1929

The Prohibition of Child Marriage Act, 2006

Prohibition of Child Marriage (Amendment) Bill 2021

Hindu Marriage Act of 1955

Gram Nyayalayas Act, 2008

Right to Education (RTE) Act 2009

73rd Constitutional Amendment Act 1992

The Cigarettes and Other tobacco products (prohibition of advertisement and regulation of trade and commerce, production, supply and distribution) act, 2003 no. 34 of 2003

Public Health Act 2007

Mahatma Gandhi National Rural Employment Guarantee Act, 2005 No. 42 OF 2005, (MGNREGA)

The Hindu succession amendment Act 2005

The National Highways Act, 1956

The Carriage by Road Act,

The Stage-Carriages Act, 1861

The Central Road and Infrastructure Fund Act, 2000

The Control of National Highways (land and traffic) Act, 2002

The Information Technology ACT, 2008

The Right to Information Act, 2005

Muslim Personal law (Shariat) Application Act 1937

JUDGMENTS OF THE COURT:

Shakti Vahini vs. Union of India & Ors. [2018] 3 SCR 770 : (2018) 7 SCC 192

Citation: WRIT PETITION (CIVIL) NO. 231 OF 2010

Vineeta Sharma Vs Rakesh Sharma (2020) 9 SCC 1DECIDED ON : 11 August 2020

Judgment on triple talak - Shayara Bano v. Union of India & Others, Writ Petition (C) No. 118 of 2016

Mohini Jain v. State of Karnataka 1992 AIR 1858

Unni Krishnan, J.P & Ors. v. State of Andhra Pradesh & Ors. 1993 AIR 217

Avinash Mehrotra v. Union of India 6 SCC 398 (2009)

Vellore Citizens Welfare Forum vs Union Of India & Ors on 28 August, 1996, AIR 1996 SC 2715: (1996) 5 SCC 647

ACTS:

Prohibition of Sati Act 1829, Sti Abolition Act

The Child Marriage Restraint Act, 1929

The Prohibition of Child Marriage Act, 2006

Prohibition of Child Marriage (Amendment) Bill 2021

Hindu Marriage Act of 1955

Gram Nyayalayas Act, 2008

Right to Education (RTE) Act 2009

73rd Constitutional Amendment Act 1992

The Cigarettes and Other tobacco products (prohibition of advertisement and regulation of trade and commerce, production, supply and distribution) act, 2003 no. 34 of 2003

Public Health Act 2007

Mahatma Gandhi National Rural Employment Guarantee Act, 2005 No. 42 OF 2005, (MGNREGA)

The Hindu succession amendment Act 2005

The National Highways Act, 1956

The Carriage by Road Act,

The Stage-Carriages Act, 1861

The Central Road and Infrastructure Fund Act, 2000

The Control of National Highways (land and traffic) Act, 2002

The Information Technology ACT, 2008

The Right to Information Act, 2005

Muslim Personal law (Shariat) Application Act 1937

JUDGMENTS OF THE COURT:

Shakti Vahini vs. Union of India & Ors. [2018] 3 SCR 770 : (2018) 7 SCC 192

Citation: WRIT PETITION (CIVIL) NO. 231 OF 2010

Vineeta Sharma Vs Rakesh Sharma (2020) 9 SCC 1DECIDED ON : 11 August 2020

Judgment on triple talak - Shayara Bano v. Union of India & Others, Writ Petition (C) No. 118 of 2016

Mohini Jain v. State of Karnataka 1992 AIR 1858

Unni Krishnan, J.P & Ors. v. State of Andhra Pradesh & Ors. 1993 AIR 217

Avinash Mehrotra v. Union of India 6 SCC 398 (2009)

Vellore Citizens Welfare Forum vs Union Of India & Ors on 28 August, 1996, AIR 1996 SC 2715: (1996) 5 SCC 647

ACTS:

Prohibition of Sati Act 1829, Sti Abolition Act

The Child Marriage Restraint Act, 1929

The Prohibition of Child Marriage Act, 2006

Prohibition of Child Marriage (Amendment) Bill 2021

Hindu Marriage Act of 1955

Gram Nyayalayas Act, 2008

Right to Education (RTE) Act 2009

73rd Constitutional Amendment Act 1992

The Cigarettes and Other tobacco products (prohibition of advertisement and regulation of trade and commerce, production, supply and distribution) act, 2003 no. 34 of 2003

Public Health Act 2007

Mahatma Gandhi National Rural Employment Guarantee Act, 2005 No. 42 OF 2005, (MGNREGA)

The Hindu succession amendment Act 2005

The National Highways Act, 1956

The Carriage by Road Act,

The Stage-Carriages Act, 1861

The Central Road and Infrastructure Fund Act, 2000

The Control of National Highways (land and traffic) Act, 2002

The Information Technology ACT, 2008

The Right to Information Act, 2005

Muslim Personal law (Shariat) Application Act 1937

JUDGMENTS OF THE COURT:

Shakti Vahini vs. Union of India & Ors. [2018] 3 SCR 770 : (2018) 7 SCC 192

Citation: WRIT PETITION (CIVIL) NO. 231 OF 2010

Vineeta Sharma Vs Rakesh Sharma (2020) 9 SCC 1DECIDED ON : 11 August 2020

Judgment on triple talak - Shayara Bano v. Union of India & Others, Writ Petition (C) No. 118 of 2016

Mohini Jain v. State of Karnataka 1992 AIR 1858

Unni Krishnan, J.P & Ors. v. State of Andhra Pradesh & Ors. 1993 AIR 217

Avinash Mehrotra v. Union of India 6 SCC 398 (2009)

Vellore Citizens Welfare Forum vs Union Of India & Ors on 28 August, 1996, AIR 1996 SC 2715: (1996) 5 SCC 647

ACTS:

Prohibition of Sati Act 1829, Sti Abolition Act

The Child Marriage Restraint Act, 1929

The Prohibition of Child Marriage Act, 2006

Prohibition of Child Marriage (Amendment) Bill 2021

Hindu Marriage Act of 1955

Gram Nyayalayas Act, 2008

Right to Education (RTE) Act 2009

73rd Constitutional Amendment Act 1992

The Cigarettes and Other tobacco products (prohibition of advertisement and regulation of trade and commerce, production, supply and distribution) act, 2003 no. 34 of 2003

Public Health Act 2007

Mahatma Gandhi National Rural Employment Guarantee Act, 2005 No. 42 OF 2005, (MGNREGA)

The Hindu succession amendment Act 2005

The National Highways Act, 1956

The Carriage by Road Act,

The Stage-Carriages Act, 1861

The Central Road and Infrastructure Fund Act, 2000

The Control of National Highways (land and traffic) Act, 2002

The Information Technology ACT, 2008

The Right to Information Act, 2005

Muslim Personal law (Shariat) Application Act 1937

JUDGMENTS OF THE COURT:

Shakti Vahini vs. Union of India & Ors. [2018] 3 SCR 770 : (2018) 7 SCC 192

Citation: WRIT PETITION (CIVIL) NO. 231 OF 2010

Vineeta Sharma Vs Rakesh Sharma (2020) 9 SCC 1DECIDED ON : 11 August 2020

Judgment on triple talak - Shayara Bano v. Union of India & Others, Writ Petition (C) No. 118 of 2016

Mohini Jain v. State of Karnataka 1992 AIR 1858

Unni Krishnan, J.P & Ors. v. State of Andhra Pradesh & Ors. 1993 AIR 217

Avinash Mehrotra v. Union of India 6 SCC 398 (2009)

Vellore Citizens Welfare Forum vs Union Of India & Ors on 28 August, 1996, AIR 1996 SC 2715: (1996) 5 SCC 647

ACTS:

Prohibition of Sati Act 1829, Sti Abolition Act

The Child Marriage Restraint Act, 1929

The Prohibition of Child Marriage Act, 2006

Prohibition of Child Marriage (Amendment) Bill 2021

Hindu Marriage Act of 1955

Gram Nyayalayas Act, 2008

Right to Education (RTE) Act 2009

73rd Constitutional Amendment Act 1992

The Cigarettes and Other tobacco products (prohibition of advertisement and regulation of trade and commerce, production, supply and distribution) act, 2003 no. 34 of 2003

Public Health Act 2007

Mahatma Gandhi National Rural Employment Guarantee Act, 2005 No. 42 OF 2005, (MGNREGA)

The Hindu succession amendment Act 2005

The National Highways Act, 1956

The Carriage by Road Act,

The Stage-Carriages Act, 1861

The Central Road and Infrastructure Fund Act, 2000

The Control of National Highways (land and traffic) Act, 2002

The Information Technology ACT, 2008

The Right to Information Act, 2005

Muslim Personal law (Shariat) Application Act 1937

JUDGMENTS OF THE COURT:

Shakti Vahini vs. Union of India & Ors. [2018] 3 SCR 770 : (2018) 7 SCC 192

Citation: WRIT PETITION (CIVIL) NO. 231 OF 2010

Vineeta Sharma Vs Rakesh Sharma (2020) 9 SCC 1DECIDED ON : 11 August 2020

Judgment on triple talak - Shayara Bano v. Union of India & Others, Writ Petition (C) No. 118 of 2016

Mohini Jain v. State of Karnataka 1992 AIR 1858

Unni Krishnan, J.P & Ors. v. State of Andhra Pradesh & Ors. 1993 AIR 217

Avinash Mehrotra v. Union of India 6 SCC 398 (2009)

Vellore Citizens Welfare Forum vs Union Of India & Ors on 28 August, 1996, AIR 1996 SC 2715: (1996) 5 SCC 647

ACTS:

Prohibition of Sati Act 1829, Sti Abolition Act

The Child Marriage Restraint Act, 1929

The Prohibition of Child Marriage Act, 2006

Prohibition of Child Marriage (Amendment) Bill 2021

Hindu Marriage Act of 1955

Gram Nyayalayas Act, 2008

Right to Education (RTE) Act 2009

73rd Constitutional Amendment Act 1992

The Cigarettes and Other tobacco products (prohibition of advertisement and regulation of trade and commerce, production, supply and distribution) act, 2003 no. 34 of 2003

Public Health Act 2007

Mahatma Gandhi National Rural Employment Guarantee Act, 2005 No. 42 OF 2005, (MGNREGA)

The Hindu succession amendment Act 2005

The National Highways Act, 1956

The Carriage by Road Act,

The Stage-Carriages Act, 1861

The Central Road and Infrastructure Fund Act, 2000

The Control of National Highways (land and traffic) Act, 2002

The Information Technology ACT, 2008

The Right to Information Act, 2005

Muslim Personal law (Shariat) Application Act 1937

JUDGMENTS OF THE COURT:

Shakti Vahini vs. Union of India & Ors. [2018] 3 SCR 770 : (2018) 7 SCC 192

Citation: WRIT PETITION (CIVIL) NO. 231 OF 2010

Vineeta Sharma Vs Rakesh Sharma (2020) 9 SCC 1DECIDED ON : 11 August 2020

Judgment on triple talak - Shayara Bano v. Union of India & Others, Writ Petition (C) No. 118 of 2016

Mohini Jain v. State of Karnataka 1992 AIR 1858

Unni Krishnan, J.P & Ors. v. State of Andhra Pradesh & Ors. 1993 AIR 217

Avinash Mehrotra v. Union of India 6 SCC 398 (2009)

Vellore Citizens Welfare Forum vs Union Of India & Ors on 28 August, 1996, AIR 1996 SC 2715: (1996) 5 SCC 647

ACTS:

Prohibition of Sati Act 1829, Sti Abolition Act

The Child Marriage Restraint Act, 1929

The Prohibition of Child Marriage Act, 2006

Prohibition of Child Marriage (Amendment) Bill 2021

Hindu Marriage Act of 1955

Gram Nyayalayas Act, 2008

Right to Education (RTE) Act 2009

73rd Constitutional Amendment Act 1992

The Cigarettes and Other tobacco products (prohibition of advertisement and regulation of trade and commerce, production, supply and distribution) act, 2003 no. 34 of 2003

Public Health Act 2007

Mahatma Gandhi National Rural Employment Guarantee Act, 2005 No. 42 OF 2005, (MGNREGA)

The Hindu succession amendment Act 2005

The National Highways Act, 1956

The Carriage by Road Act,

The Stage-Carriages Act, 1861

The Central Road and Infrastructure Fund Act, 2000

The Control of National Highways (land and traffic) Act, 2002

The Information Technology ACT, 2008

The Right to Information Act, 2005

Muslim Personal law (Shariat) Application Act 1937

JUDGMENTS OF THE COURT:

Shakti Vahini vs. Union of India & Ors. [2018] 3 SCR 770 : (2018) 7 SCC 192

Citation: WRIT PETITION (CIVIL) NO. 231 OF 2010

Vineeta Sharma Vs Rakesh Sharma (2020) 9 SCC 1DECIDED ON : 11 August 2020

Judgment on triple talak - Shayara Bano v. Union of India & Others, Writ Petition (C) No. 118 of 2016

Mohini Jain v. State of Karnataka 1992 AIR 1858

Unni Krishnan, J.P & Ors. v. State of Andhra Pradesh & Ors. 1993 AIR 217

Avinash Mehrotra v. Union of India 6 SCC 398 (2009)

Vellore Citizens Welfare Forum vs Union Of India & Ors on 28 August, 1996, AIR 1996 SC 2715: (1996) 5 SCC 647

ACTS:

Prohibition of Sati Act 1829, Sti Abolition Act

The Child Marriage Restraint Act, 1929

The Prohibition of Child Marriage Act, 2006

Prohibition of Child Marriage (Amendment) Bill 2021

Hindu Marriage Act of 1955

Gram Nyayalayas Act, 2008

Right to Education (RTE) Act 2009

73rd Constitutional Amendment Act 1992

The Cigarettes and Other tobacco products (prohibition of advertisement and regulation of trade and commerce, production, supply and distribution) act, 2003 no. 34 of 2003

Public Health Act 2007

Mahatma Gandhi National Rural Employment Guarantee Act, 2005 No. 42 OF 2005, (MGNREGA)

The Hindu succession amendment Act 2005

The National Highways Act, 1956

The Carriage by Road Act,

The Stage-Carriages Act, 1861

The Central Road and Infrastructure Fund Act, 2000

The Control of National Highways (land and traffic) Act, 2002

The Information Technology ACT, 2008

The Right to Information Act, 2005

Muslim Personal law (Shariat) Application Act 1937

JUDGMENTS OF THE COURT:

Shakti Vahini vs. Union of India & Ors. [2018] 3 SCR 770 : (2018) 7 SCC 192

Citation: WRIT PETITION (CIVIL) NO. 231 OF 2010

Vineeta Sharma Vs Rakesh Sharma (2020) 9 SCC 1DECIDED ON : 11 August 2020

Judgment on triple talak - Shayara Bano v. Union of India & Others, Writ Petition (C) No. 118 of 2016

Mohini Jain v. State of Karnataka 1992 AIR 1858

Unni Krishnan, J.P & Ors. v. State of Andhra Pradesh & Ors. 1993 AIR 217

Avinash Mehrotra v. Union of India 6 SCC 398 (2009)

Vellore Citizens Welfare Forum vs Union Of India & Ors on 28 August, 1996, AIR 1996 SC 2715: (1996) 5 SCC 647

ACTS:

Prohibition of Sati Act 1829, Sti Abolition Act

The Child Marriage Restraint Act, 1929

The Prohibition of Child Marriage Act, 2006

Prohibition of Child Marriage (Amendment) Bill 2021

Hindu Marriage Act of 1955

Gram Nyayalayas Act, 2008

Right to Education (RTE) Act 2009

73rd Constitutional Amendment Act 1992

The Cigarettes and Other tobacco products (prohibition of advertisement and regulation of trade and commerce, production, supply and distribution) act, 2003 no. 34 of 2003

Public Health Act 2007

Mahatma Gandhi National Rural Employment Guarantee Act, 2005 No. 42 OF 2005, (MGNREGA)

The Hindu succession amendment Act 2005

The National Highways Act, 1956

The Carriage by Road Act,

The Stage-Carriages Act, 1861

The Central Road and Infrastructure Fund Act, 2000

The Control of National Highways (land and traffic) Act, 2002

The Information Technology ACT, 2008

The Right to Information Act, 2005

Muslim Personal law (Shariat) Application Act 1937

JUDGMENTS OF THE COURT:

Shakti Vahini vs. Union of India & Ors. [2018] 3 SCR 770 : (2018) 7 SCC 192

Citation: WRIT PETITION (CIVIL) NO. 231 OF 2010

Vineeta Sharma Vs Rakesh Sharma (2020) 9 SCC 1DECIDED ON : 11 August 2020

Judgment on triple talak - Shayara Bano v. Union of India & Others, Writ Petition (C) No. 118 of 2016

Mohini Jain v. State of Karnataka 1992 AIR 1858

Unni Krishnan, J.P & Ors. v. State of Andhra Pradesh & Ors. 1993 AIR 217

Avinash Mehrotra v. Union of India 6 SCC 398 (2009)

Vellore Citizens Welfare Forum vs Union Of India & Ors on 28 August, 1996, AIR 1996 SC 2715: (1996) 5 SCC 647

ACTS:

Prohibition of Sati Act 1829, Sti Abolition Act

The Child Marriage Restraint Act, 1929

The Prohibition of Child Marriage Act, 2006

Prohibition of Child Marriage (Amendment) Bill 2021

Hindu Marriage Act of 1955

Gram Nyayalayas Act, 2008

Right to Education (RTE) Act 2009

73rd Constitutional Amendment Act 1992

The Cigarettes and Other tobacco products (prohibition of advertisement and regulation of trade and commerce, production, supply and distribution) act, 2003 no. 34 of 2003

Public Health Act 2007

Mahatma Gandhi National Rural Employment Guarantee Act, 2005 No. 42 OF 2005, (MGNREGA)

The Hindu succession amendment Act 2005

The National Highways Act, 1956

The Carriage by Road Act,

The Stage-Carriages Act, 1861

The Central Road and Infrastructure Fund Act, 2000

The Control of National Highways (land and traffic) Act, 2002

The Information Technology ACT, 2008

The Right to Information Act, 2005

Muslim Personal law (Shariat) Application Act 1937

JUDGMENTS OF THE COURT:

Shakti Vahini vs. Union of India & Ors. [2018] 3 SCR 770 : (2018) 7 SCC 192

Citation: WRIT PETITION (CIVIL) NO. 231 OF 2010

Vineeta Sharma Vs Rakesh Sharma (2020) 9 SCC 1DECIDED ON : 11 August 2020

Judgment on triple talak - Shayara Bano v. Union of India & Others, Writ Petition (C) No. 118 of 2016

Mohini Jain v. State of Karnataka 1992 AIR 1858

Unni Krishnan, J.P & Ors. v. State of Andhra Pradesh & Ors. 1993 AIR 217

Avinash Mehrotra v. Union of India 6 SCC 398 (2009)

Vellore Citizens Welfare Forum vs Union Of India & Ors on 28 August, 1996, AIR 1996 SC 2715: (1996) 5 SCC 647

ACTS:

Prohibition of Sati Act 1829, Sti Abolition Act

The Child Marriage Restraint Act, 1929

The Prohibition of Child Marriage Act, 2006

Prohibition of Child Marriage (Amendment) Bill 2021

Hindu Marriage Act of 1955

Gram Nyayalayas Act, 2008

Right to Education (RTE) Act 2009

73rd Constitutional Amendment Act 1992

The Cigarettes and Other tobacco products (prohibition of advertisement and regulation of trade and commerce, production, supply and distribution) act, 2003 no. 34 of 2003

Public Health Act 2007

Mahatma Gandhi National Rural Employment Guarantee Act, 2005 No. 42 OF 2005, (MGNREGA)

The Hindu succession amendment Act 2005

The National Highways Act, 1956

The Carriage by Road Act,

The Stage-Carriages Act, 1861

The Central Road and Infrastructure Fund Act, 2000

The Control of National Highways (land and traffic) Act, 2002

The Information Technology ACT, 2008

The Right to Information Act, 2005

Muslim Personal law (Shariat) Application Act 1937

JUDGMENTS OF THE COURT:

Shakti Vahini vs. Union of India & Ors. [2018] 3 SCR 770 : (2018) 7 SCC 192

Citation: WRIT PETITION (CIVIL) NO. 231 OF 2010

Vineeta Sharma Vs Rakesh Sharma (2020) 9 SCC 1DECIDED ON : 11 August 2020

Judgment on triple talak - Shayara Bano v. Union of India & Others, Writ Petition (C) No. 118 of 2016

Mohini Jain v. State of Karnataka 1992 AIR 1858

Unni Krishnan, J.P & Ors. v. State of Andhra Pradesh & Ors. 1993 AIR 217

Avinash Mehrotra v. Union of India 6 SCC 398 (2009)

Vellore Citizens Welfare Forum vs Union Of India & Ors on 28 August, 1996, AIR 1996 SC 2715: (1996) 5 SCC 647

ACTS:

Prohibition of Sati Act 1829, Sti Abolition Act

The Child Marriage Restraint Act, 1929

The Prohibition of Child Marriage Act, 2006

Prohibition of Child Marriage (Amendment) Bill 2021

Hindu Marriage Act of 1955

Gram Nyayalayas Act, 2008

Right to Education (RTE) Act 2009

73rd Constitutional Amendment Act 1992

The Cigarettes and Other tobacco products (prohibition of advertisement and regulation of trade and commerce, production, supply and distribution) act, 2003 no. 34 of 2003

Public Health Act 2007

Mahatma Gandhi National Rural Employment Guarantee Act, 2005 No. 42 OF 2005, (MGNREGA)

The Hindu succession amendment Act 2005

The National Highways Act, 1956

The Carriage by Road Act,

The Stage-Carriages Act, 1861

The Central Road and Infrastructure Fund Act, 2000

The Control of National Highways (land and traffic) Act, 2002

The Information Technology ACT, 2008

The Right to Information Act, 2005

Muslim Personal law (Shariat) Application Act 1937

JUDGMENTS OF THE COURT:

Shakti Vahini vs. Union of India & Ors. [2018] 3 SCR 770 : (2018) 7 SCC 192

Citation: WRIT PETITION (CIVIL) NO. 231 OF 2010

Vineeta Sharma Vs Rakesh Sharma (2020) 9 SCC 1DECIDED ON : 11 August 2020

Judgment on triple talak - Shayara Bano v. Union of India & Others, Writ Petition (C) No. 118 of 2016

Mohini Jain v. State of Karnataka 1992 AIR 1858

Unni Krishnan, J.P & Ors. v. State of Andhra Pradesh & Ors. 1993 AIR 217

Avinash Mehrotra v. Union of India 6 SCC 398 (2009)

Vellore Citizens Welfare Forum vs Union Of India & Ors on 28 August, 1996, AIR 1996 SC 2715: (1996) 5 SCC 647

ACTS:

Prohibition of Sati Act 1829, Sti Abolition Act

The Child Marriage Restraint Act, 1929

The Prohibition of Child Marriage Act, 2006

Prohibition of Child Marriage (Amendment) Bill 2021

Hindu Marriage Act of 1955

Gram Nyayalayas Act, 2008

Right to Education (RTE) Act 2009

73rd Constitutional Amendment Act 1992

The Cigarettes and Other tobacco products (prohibition of advertisement and regulation of trade and commerce, production, supply and distribution) act, 2003 no. 34 of 2003

Public Health Act 2007

Mahatma Gandhi National Rural Employment Guarantee Act, 2005 No. 42 OF 2005, (MGNREGA)

The Hindu succession amendment Act 2005

The National Highways Act, 1956

The Carriage by Road Act,

The Stage-Carriages Act, 1861

The Central Road and Infrastructure Fund Act, 2000

The Control of National Highways (land and traffic) Act, 2002

The Information Technology ACT, 2008

The Right to Information Act, 2005

Muslim Personal law (Shariat) Application Act 1937

JUDGMENTS OF THE COURT:

Shakti Vahini vs. Union of India & Ors. [2018] 3 SCR 770 : (2018) 7 SCC 192

Citation: WRIT PETITION (CIVIL) NO. 231 OF 2010

Vineeta Sharma Vs Rakesh Sharma (2020) 9 SCC 1DECIDED ON : 11 August 2020

Judgment on triple talak - Shayara Bano v. Union of India & Others, Writ Petition (C) No. 118 of 2016

Mohini Jain v. State of Karnataka 1992 AIR 1858

Unni Krishnan, J.P & Ors. v. State of Andhra Pradesh & Ors. 1993 AIR 217

Avinash Mehrotra v. Union of India 6 SCC 398 (2009)

Vellore Citizens Welfare Forum vs Union Of India & Ors on 28 August, 1996, AIR 1996 SC 2715: (1996) 5 SCC 647

ACTS:

Prohibition of Sati Act 1829, Sti Abolition Act

The Child Marriage Restraint Act, 1929

The Prohibition of Child Marriage Act, 2006

Prohibition of Child Marriage (Amendment) Bill 2021

Hindu Marriage Act of 1955

Gram Nyayalayas Act, 2008

Right to Education (RTE) Act 2009

73[rd] Constitutional Amendment Act 1992

The Cigarettes and Other tobacco products (prohibition of advertisement and regulation of trade and commerce, production, supply and distribution) act, 2003 no. 34 of 2003

Public Health Act 2007

Mahatma Gandhi National Rural Employment Guarantee Act, 2005 No. 42 OF 2005, (MGNREGA)

The Hindu succession amendment Act 2005

The National Highways Act, 1956

The Carriage by Road Act,

The Stage-Carriages Act, 1861

The Central Road and Infrastructure Fund Act, 2000

The Control of National Highways (land and traffic) Act, 2002

The Information Technology ACT, 2008

The Right to Information Act, 2005

Muslim Personal law (Shariat) Application Act 1937

JUDGMENTS OF THE COURT:

Shakti Vahini vs. Union of India & Ors. [2018] 3 SCR 770 : (2018) 7 SCC 192

Citation: WRIT PETITION (CIVIL) NO. 231 OF 2010

Vineeta Sharma Vs Rakesh Sharma (2020) 9 SCC 1DECIDED ON : 11 August 2020

Judgment on triple talak - Shayara Bano v. Union of India & Others, Writ Petition (C) No. 118 of 2016

Mohini Jain v. State of Karnataka 1992 AIR 1858

Unni Krishnan, J.P & Ors. v. State of Andhra Pradesh & Ors. 1993 AIR 217

Avinash Mehrotra v. Union of India 6 SCC 398 (2009)

Vellore Citizens Welfare Forum vs Union Of India & Ors on 28 August, 1996, AIR 1996 SC 2715: (1996) 5 SCC 647

ACTS:

Prohibition of Sati Act 1829, Sti Abolition Act

The Child Marriage Restraint Act, 1929

The Prohibition of Child Marriage Act, 2006

Prohibition of Child Marriage (Amendment) Bill 2021

Hindu Marriage Act of 1955

Gram Nyayalayas Act, 2008

Right to Education (RTE) Act 2009

73rd Constitutional Amendment Act 1992

The Cigarettes and Other tobacco products (prohibition of advertisement and regulation of trade and commerce, production, supply and distribution) act, 2003 no. 34 of 2003

Public Health Act 2007

Mahatma Gandhi National Rural Employment Guarantee Act, 2005 No. 42 OF 2005, (MGNREGA)

The Hindu succession amendment Act 2005

The National Highways Act, 1956

The Carriage by Road Act,

The Stage-Carriages Act, 1861

The Central Road and Infrastructure Fund Act, 2000

The Control of National Highways (land and traffic) Act, 2002

The Information Technology ACT, 2008

The Right to Information Act, 2005

Muslim Personal law (Shariat) Application Act 1937

JUDGMENTS OF THE COURT:

Shakti Vahini vs. Union of India & Ors. [2018] 3 SCR 770 : (2018) 7 SCC 192

Citation: WRIT PETITION (CIVIL) NO. 231 OF 2010

Vineeta Sharma Vs Rakesh Sharma (2020) 9 SCC 1DECIDED ON : 11 August 2020

Judgment on triple talak - Shayara Bano v. Union of India & Others, Writ Petition (C) No. 118 of 2016

Mohini Jain v. State of Karnataka 1992 AIR 1858

Unni Krishnan, J.P & Ors. v. State of Andhra Pradesh & Ors. 1993 AIR 217

Avinash Mehrotra v. Union of India 6 SCC 398 (2009)

Vellore Citizens Welfare Forum vs Union Of India & Ors on 28 August, 1996, AIR 1996 SC 2715: (1996) 5 SCC 647

ACTS:

Prohibition of Sati Act 1829, Sti Abolition Act

The Child Marriage Restraint Act, 1929

The Prohibition of Child Marriage Act, 2006

Prohibition of Child Marriage (Amendment) Bill 2021

Hindu Marriage Act of 1955

Gram Nyayalayas Act, 2008

Right to Education (RTE) Act 2009

73rd Constitutional Amendment Act 1992

The Cigarettes and Other tobacco products (prohibition of advertisement and regulation of trade and commerce, production, supply and distribution) act, 2003 no. 34 of 2003

Public Health Act 2007

Mahatma Gandhi National Rural Employment Guarantee Act, 2005 No. 42 OF 2005, (MGNREGA)

The Hindu succession amendment Act 2005

The National Highways Act, 1956

The Carriage by Road Act,

The Stage-Carriages Act, 1861

The Central Road and Infrastructure Fund Act, 2000

The Control of National Highways (land and traffic) Act, 2002

The Information Technology ACT, 2008

The Right to Information Act, 2005

Muslim Personal law (Shariat) Application Act 1937

JUDGMENTS OF THE COURT:

Shakti Vahini vs. Union of India & Ors. [2018] 3 SCR 770 : (2018) 7 SCC 192

Citation: WRIT PETITION (CIVIL) NO. 231 OF 2010

Vineeta Sharma Vs Rakesh Sharma (2020) 9 SCC 1DECIDED ON : 11 August 2020

Judgment on triple talak - Shayara Bano v. Union of India & Others, Writ Petition (C) No. 118 of 2016

Mohini Jain v. State of Karnataka 1992 AIR 1858

Unni Krishnan, J.P & Ors. v. State of Andhra Pradesh & Ors. 1993 AIR 217

Avinash Mehrotra v. Union of India 6 SCC 398 (2009)

Vellore Citizens Welfare Forum vs Union Of India & Ors on 28 August, 1996, AIR 1996 SC 2715: (1996) 5 SCC 647

ACTS:

Prohibition of Sati Act 1829, Sti Abolition Act

The Child Marriage Restraint Act, 1929

The Prohibition of Child Marriage Act, 2006

Prohibition of Child Marriage (Amendment) Bill 2021

Hindu Marriage Act of 1955

Gram Nyayalayas Act, 2008

Right to Education (RTE) Act 2009

73rd Constitutional Amendment Act 1992

The Cigarettes and Other tobacco products (prohibition of advertisement and regulation of trade and commerce, production, supply and distribution) act, 2003 no. 34 of 2003

Public Health Act 2007

Mahatma Gandhi National Rural Employment Guarantee Act, 2005 No. 42 OF 2005, (MGNREGA)

The Hindu succession amendment Act 2005

The National Highways Act, 1956

The Carriage by Road Act,

The Stage-Carriages Act, 1861

The Central Road and Infrastructure Fund Act, 2000

The Control of National Highways (land and traffic) Act, 2002

The Information Technology ACT, 2008

The Right to Information Act, 2005

Muslim Personal law (Shariat) Application Act 1937

JUDGMENTS OF THE COURT:

Shakti Vahini vs. Union of India & Ors. [2018] 3 SCR 770 : (2018) 7 SCC 192

Citation: WRIT PETITION (CIVIL) NO. 231 OF 2010

Vineeta Sharma Vs Rakesh Sharma (2020) 9 SCC 1DECIDED ON : 11 August 2020

Judgment on triple talak - Shayara Bano v. Union of India & Others, Writ Petition (C) No. 118 of 2016

Mohini Jain v. State of Karnataka 1992 AIR 1858

Unni Krishnan, J.P & Ors. v. State of Andhra Pradesh & Ors. 1993 AIR 217

Avinash Mehrotra v. Union of India 6 SCC 398 (2009)

Vellore Citizens Welfare Forum vs Union Of India & Ors on 28 August, 1996, AIR 1996 SC 2715: (1996) 5 SCC 647

ACTS:

Prohibition of Sati Act 1829, Sti Abolition Act

The Child Marriage Restraint Act, 1929

The Prohibition of Child Marriage Act, 2006

Prohibition of Child Marriage (Amendment) Bill 2021

Hindu Marriage Act of 1955

Gram Nyayalayas Act, 2008

Right to Education (RTE) Act 2009

73rd Constitutional Amendment Act 1992

The Cigarettes and Other tobacco products (prohibition of advertisement and regulation of trade and commerce, production, supply and distribution) act, 2003 no. 34 of 2003

Public Health Act 2007

Mahatma Gandhi National Rural Employment Guarantee Act, 2005 No. 42 OF 2005, (MGNREGA)

The Hindu succession amendment Act 2005

The National Highways Act, 1956

The Carriage by Road Act,

The Stage-Carriages Act, 1861

The Central Road and Infrastructure Fund Act, 2000

The Control of National Highways (land and traffic) Act, 2002

The Information Technology ACT, 2008

The Right to Information Act, 2005

Muslim Personal law (Shariat) Application Act 1937

JUDGMENTS OF THE COURT:

Shakti Vahini vs. Union of India & Ors. [2018] 3 SCR 770 : (2018) 7 SCC 192

Citation: WRIT PETITION (CIVIL) NO. 231 OF 2010

Vineeta Sharma Vs Rakesh Sharma (2020) 9 SCC 1DECIDED ON : 11 August 2020

Judgment on triple talak - Shayara Bano v. Union of India & Others, Writ Petition (C) No. 118 of 2016

Mohini Jain v. State of Karnataka 1992 AIR 1858

Unni Krishnan, J.P & Ors. v. State of Andhra Pradesh & Ors. 1993 AIR 217

Avinash Mehrotra v. Union of India 6 SCC 398 (2009)

Vellore Citizens Welfare Forum vs Union Of India & Ors on 28 August, 1996, AIR 1996 SC 2715: (1996) 5 SCC 647

ACTS:

Prohibition of Sati Act 1829, Sti Abolition Act

The Child Marriage Restraint Act, 1929

The Prohibition of Child Marriage Act, 2006

Prohibition of Child Marriage (Amendment) Bill 2021

Hindu Marriage Act of 1955

Gram Nyayalayas Act, 2008

Right to Education (RTE) Act 2009

73rd Constitutional Amendment Act 1992

The Cigarettes and Other tobacco products (prohibition of advertisement and regulation of trade and commerce, production, supply and distribution) act, 2003 no. 34 of 2003

Public Health Act 2007

Mahatma Gandhi National Rural Employment Guarantee Act, 2005 No. 42 OF 2005, (MGNREGA)

The Hindu succession amendment Act 2005

The National Highways Act, 1956

The Carriage by Road Act,

The Stage-Carriages Act, 1861

The Central Road and Infrastructure Fund Act, 2000

The Control of National Highways (land and traffic) Act, 2002

The Information Technology ACT, 2008

The Right to Information Act, 2005

Muslim Personal law (Shariat) Application Act 1937

JUDGMENTS OF THE COURT:

Shakti Vahini vs. Union of India & Ors. [2018] 3 SCR 770 : (2018) 7 SCC 192

Citation: WRIT PETITION (CIVIL) NO. 231 OF 2010

Vineeta Sharma Vs Rakesh Sharma (2020) 9 SCC 1DECIDED ON : 11 August 2020

Judgment on triple talak - Shayara Bano v. Union of India & Others, Writ Petition (C) No. 118 of 2016

Mohini Jain v. State of Karnataka 1992 AIR 1858

Unni Krishnan, J.P & Ors. v. State of Andhra Pradesh & Ors. 1993 AIR 217

Avinash Mehrotra v. Union of India 6 SCC 398 (2009)

Vellore Citizens Welfare Forum vs Union Of India & Ors on 28 August, 1996, AIR 1996 SC 2715: (1996) 5 SCC 647

ACTS:

Prohibition of Sati Act 1829, Sti Abolition Act

The Child Marriage Restraint Act, 1929

The Prohibition of Child Marriage Act, 2006

Prohibition of Child Marriage (Amendment) Bill 2021

Hindu Marriage Act of 1955

Gram Nyayalayas Act, 2008

Right to Education (RTE) Act 2009

73rd Constitutional Amendment Act 1992

The Cigarettes and Other tobacco products (prohibition of advertisement and regulation of trade and commerce, production, supply and distribution) act, 2003 no. 34 of 2003

Public Health Act 2007

Mahatma Gandhi National Rural Employment Guarantee Act, 2005 No. 42 OF 2005, (MGNREGA)

The Hindu succession amendment Act 2005

The National Highways Act, 1956

The Carriage by Road Act,

The Stage-Carriages Act, 1861

The Central Road and Infrastructure Fund Act, 2000

The Control of National Highways (land and traffic) Act, 2002

The Information Technology ACT, 2008

The Right to Information Act, 2005

Muslim Personal law (Shariat) Application Act 1937

JUDGMENTS OF THE COURT:

Shakti Vahini vs. Union of India & Ors. [2018] 3 SCR 770 : (2018) 7 SCC 192

Citation: WRIT PETITION (CIVIL) NO. 231 OF 2010

Vineeta Sharma Vs Rakesh Sharma (2020) 9 SCC 1DECIDED ON : 11 August 2020

Judgment on triple talak - Shayara Bano v. Union of India & Others, Writ Petition (C) No. 118 of 2016

Mohini Jain v. State of Karnataka 1992 AIR 1858

Unni Krishnan, J.P & Ors. v. State of Andhra Pradesh & Ors. 1993 AIR 217

Avinash Mehrotra v. Union of India 6 SCC 398 (2009)

Vellore Citizens Welfare Forum vs Union Of India & Ors on 28 August, 1996, AIR 1996 SC 2715: (1996) 5 SCC 647

ACTS:

Prohibition of Sati Act 1829, Sti Abolition Act

The Child Marriage Restraint Act, 1929

The Prohibition of Child Marriage Act, 2006

Prohibition of Child Marriage (Amendment) Bill 2021

Hindu Marriage Act of 1955

Gram Nyayalayas Act, 2008

Right to Education (RTE) Act 2009

73rd Constitutional Amendment Act 1992

The Cigarettes and Other tobacco products (prohibition of advertisement and regulation of trade and commerce, production, supply and distribution) act, 2003 no. 34 of 2003

Public Health Act 2007

Mahatma Gandhi National Rural Employment Guarantee Act, 2005 No. 42 OF 2005, (MGNREGA)

The Hindu succession amendment Act 2005

The National Highways Act, 1956

The Carriage by Road Act,

The Stage-Carriages Act, 1861

The Central Road and Infrastructure Fund Act, 2000

The Control of National Highways (land and traffic) Act, 2002

The Information Technology ACT, 2008

The Right to Information Act, 2005

Muslim Personal law (Shariat) Application Act 1937

JUDGMENTS OF THE COURT:

Shakti Vahini vs. Union of India & Ors. [2018] 3 SCR 770 : (2018) 7 SCC 192

Citation: WRIT PETITION (CIVIL) NO. 231 OF 2010

Vineeta Sharma Vs Rakesh Sharma (2020) 9 SCC 1DECIDED ON : 11 August 2020

Judgment on triple talak - Shayara Bano v. Union of India & Others, Writ Petition (C) No. 118 of 2016

Mohini Jain v. State of Karnataka 1992 AIR 1858

Unni Krishnan, J.P & Ors. v. State of Andhra Pradesh & Ors. 1993 AIR 217

Avinash Mehrotra v. Union of India 6 SCC 398 (2009)

Vellore Citizens Welfare Forum vs Union Of India & Ors on 28 August, 1996, AIR 1996 SC 2715: (1996) 5 SCC 647

ACTS:

Prohibition of Sati Act 1829, Sti Abolition Act

The Child Marriage Restraint Act, 1929

The Prohibition of Child Marriage Act, 2006

Prohibition of Child Marriage (Amendment) Bill 2021

Hindu Marriage Act of 1955

Gram Nyayalayas Act, 2008

Right to Education (RTE) Act 2009

73rd Constitutional Amendment Act 1992

The Cigarettes and Other tobacco products (prohibition of advertisement and regulation of trade and commerce, production, supply and distribution) act, 2003 no. 34 of 2003

Public Health Act 2007

Mahatma Gandhi National Rural Employment Guarantee Act, 2005 No. 42 OF 2005, (MGNREGA)

The Hindu succession amendment Act 2005

The National Highways Act, 1956

The Carriage by Road Act,

The Stage-Carriages Act, 1861

The Central Road and Infrastructure Fund Act, 2000

The Control of National Highways (land and traffic) Act, 2002

The Information Technology ACT, 2008

The Right to Information Act, 2005

Muslim Personal law (Shariat) Application Act 1937

JUDGMENTS OF THE COURT:

Shakti Vahini vs. Union of India & Ors. [2018] 3 SCR 770 : (2018) 7 SCC 192

Citation: WRIT PETITION (CIVIL) NO. 231 OF 2010

Vineeta Sharma Vs Rakesh Sharma (2020) 9 SCC 1DECIDED ON : 11 August 2020

Judgment on triple talak - Shayara Bano v. Union of India & Others, Writ Petition (C) No. 118 of 2016

Mohini Jain v. State of Karnataka 1992 AIR 1858

Unni Krishnan, J.P & Ors. v. State of Andhra Pradesh & Ors. 1993 AIR 217

Avinash Mehrotra v. Union of India 6 SCC 398 (2009)

Vellore Citizens Welfare Forum vs Union Of India & Ors on 28 August, 1996, AIR 1996 SC 2715: (1996) 5 SCC 647

ACTS:

Prohibition of Sati Act 1829, Sti Abolition Act

The Child Marriage Restraint Act, 1929

The Prohibition of Child Marriage Act, 2006

Prohibition of Child Marriage (Amendment) Bill 2021

Hindu Marriage Act of 1955

Gram Nyayalayas Act, 2008

Right to Education (RTE) Act 2009

73rd Constitutional Amendment Act 1992

The Cigarettes and Other tobacco products (prohibition of advertisement and regulation of trade and commerce, production, supply and distribution) act, 2003 no. 34 of 2003

Public Health Act 2007

Mahatma Gandhi National Rural Employment Guarantee Act, 2005 No. 42 OF 2005, (MGNREGA)

The Hindu succession amendment Act 2005

The National Highways Act, 1956

The Carriage by Road Act,

The Stage-Carriages Act, 1861

The Central Road and Infrastructure Fund Act, 2000

The Control of National Highways (land and traffic) Act, 2002

The Information Technology ACT, 2008

The Right to Information Act, 2005

Muslim Personal law (Shariat) Application Act 1937

JUDGMENTS OF THE COURT:

Shakti Vahini vs. Union of India & Ors. [2018] 3 SCR 770 : (2018) 7 SCC 192

Citation: WRIT PETITION (CIVIL) NO. 231 OF 2010

Vineeta Sharma Vs Rakesh Sharma (2020) 9 SCC 1DECIDED ON : 11 August 2020

Judgment on triple talak - Shayara Bano v. Union of India & Others, Writ Petition (C) No. 118 of 2016

Mohini Jain v. State of Karnataka 1992 AIR 1858

Unni Krishnan, J.P & Ors. v. State of Andhra Pradesh & Ors. 1993 AIR 217

Avinash Mehrotra v. Union of India 6 SCC 398 (2009)

Vellore Citizens Welfare Forum vs Union Of India & Ors on 28 August, 1996, AIR 1996 SC 2715: (1996) 5 SCC 647

ACTS:

Prohibition of Sati Act 1829, Sti Abolition Act

The Child Marriage Restraint Act, 1929

The Prohibition of Child Marriage Act, 2006

Prohibition of Child Marriage (Amendment) Bill 2021

Hindu Marriage Act of 1955

Gram Nyayalayas Act, 2008

Right to Education (RTE) Act 2009

73rd Constitutional Amendment Act 1992

The Cigarettes and Other tobacco products (prohibition of advertisement and regulation of trade and commerce, production, supply and distribution) act, 2003 no. 34 of 2003

Public Health Act 2007

Mahatma Gandhi National Rural Employment Guarantee Act, 2005 No. 42 OF 2005, (MGNREGA)

The Hindu succession amendment Act 2005

The National Highways Act, 1956

The Carriage by Road Act,

The Stage-Carriages Act, 1861

The Central Road and Infrastructure Fund Act, 2000

The Control of National Highways (land and traffic) Act, 2002

The Information Technology ACT, 2008

The Right to Information Act, 2005

Muslim Personal law (Shariat) Application Act 1937

JUDGMENTS OF THE COURT:

Shakti Vahini vs. Union of India & Ors. [2018] 3 SCR 770 : (2018) 7 SCC 192

Citation: WRIT PETITION (CIVIL) NO. 231 OF 2010

Vineeta Sharma Vs Rakesh Sharma (2020) 9 SCC 1DECIDED ON : 11 August 2020

Judgment on triple talak - Shayara Bano v. Union of India & Others, Writ Petition (C) No. 118 of 2016

Mohini Jain v. State of Karnataka 1992 AIR 1858

Unni Krishnan, J.P & Ors. v. State of Andhra Pradesh & Ors. 1993 AIR 217

Avinash Mehrotra v. Union of India 6 SCC 398 (2009)

Vellore Citizens Welfare Forum vs Union Of India & Ors on 28 August, 1996, AIR 1996 SC 2715: (1996) 5 SCC 647

ACTS:

Prohibition of Sati Act 1829, Sti Abolition Act

The Child Marriage Restraint Act, 1929

The Prohibition of Child Marriage Act, 2006

Prohibition of Child Marriage (Amendment) Bill 2021

Hindu Marriage Act of 1955

Gram Nyayalayas Act, 2008

Right to Education (RTE) Act 2009

73rd Constitutional Amendment Act 1992

The Cigarettes and Other tobacco products (prohibition of advertisement and regulation of trade and commerce, production, supply and distribution) act, 2003 no. 34 of 2003

Public Health Act 2007

Mahatma Gandhi National Rural Employment Guarantee Act, 2005 No. 42 OF 2005, (MGNREGA)

The Hindu succession amendment Act 2005

The National Highways Act, 1956

The Carriage by Road Act,

The Stage-Carriages Act, 1861

The Central Road and Infrastructure Fund Act, 2000

The Control of National Highways (land and traffic) Act, 2002

The Information Technology ACT, 2008

The Right to Information Act, 2005

Muslim Personal law (Shariat) Application Act 1937

JUDGMENTS OF THE COURT:

Shakti Vahini vs. Union of India & Ors. [2018] 3 SCR 770 : (2018) 7 SCC 192

Citation: WRIT PETITION (CIVIL) NO. 231 OF 2010

Vineeta Sharma Vs Rakesh Sharma (2020) 9 SCC 1DECIDED ON : 11 August 2020

Judgment on triple talak - Shayara Bano v. Union of India & Others, Writ Petition (C) No. 118 of 2016

Mohini Jain v. State of Karnataka 1992 AIR 1858

Unni Krishnan, J.P & Ors. v. State of Andhra Pradesh & Ors. 1993 AIR 217

Avinash Mehrotra v. Union of India 6 SCC 398 (2009)

Vellore Citizens Welfare Forum vs Union Of India & Ors on 28 August, 1996, AIR 1996 SC 2715: (1996) 5 SCC 647

ACTS:

Prohibition of Sati Act 1829, Sti Abolition Act

The Child Marriage Restraint Act, 1929

The Prohibition of Child Marriage Act, 2006

Prohibition of Child Marriage (Amendment) Bill 2021

Hindu Marriage Act of 1955

Gram Nyayalayas Act, 2008

Right to Education (RTE) Act 2009

73rd Constitutional Amendment Act 1992

The Cigarettes and Other tobacco products (prohibition of advertisement and regulation of trade and commerce, production, supply and distribution) act, 2003 no. 34 of 2003

Public Health Act 2007

Mahatma Gandhi National Rural Employment Guarantee Act, 2005 No. 42 OF 2005, (MGNREGA)

The Hindu succession amendment Act 2005

The National Highways Act, 1956

The Carriage by Road Act,

The Stage-Carriages Act, 1861

The Central Road and Infrastructure Fund Act, 2000

The Control of National Highways (land and traffic) Act, 2002

The Information Technology ACT, 2008

The Right to Information Act, 2005

Muslim Personal law (Shariat) Application Act 1937

JUDGMENTS OF THE COURT:

Shakti Vahini vs. Union of India & Ors. [2018] 3 SCR 770 : (2018) 7 SCC 192

Citation: WRIT PETITION (CIVIL) NO. 231 OF 2010

Vineeta Sharma Vs Rakesh Sharma (2020) 9 SCC 1DECIDED ON : 11 August 2020

Judgment on triple talak - Shayara Bano v. Union of India & Others, Writ Petition (C) No. 118 of 2016

Mohini Jain v. State of Karnataka 1992 AIR 1858

Unni Krishnan, J.P & Ors. v. State of Andhra Pradesh & Ors. 1993 AIR 217

Avinash Mehrotra v. Union of India 6 SCC 398 (2009)

Vellore Citizens Welfare Forum vs Union Of India & Ors on 28 August, 1996, AIR 1996 SC 2715: (1996) 5 SCC 647

ACTS:

Prohibition of Sati Act 1829, Sti Abolition Act

The Child Marriage Restraint Act, 1929

The Prohibition of Child Marriage Act, 2006

Prohibition of Child Marriage (Amendment) Bill 2021

Hindu Marriage Act of 1955

Gram Nyayalayas Act, 2008

Right to Education (RTE) Act 2009

73rd Constitutional Amendment Act 1992

The Cigarettes and Other tobacco products (prohibition of advertisement and regulation of trade and commerce, production, supply and distribution) act, 2003 no. 34 of 2003

Public Health Act 2007

Mahatma Gandhi National Rural Employment Guarantee Act, 2005 No. 42 OF 2005, (MGNREGA)

The Hindu succession amendment Act 2005

The National Highways Act, 1956

The Carriage by Road Act,

The Stage-Carriages Act, 1861

The Central Road and Infrastructure Fund Act, 2000

The Control of National Highways (land and traffic) Act, 2002

The Information Technology ACT, 2008

The Right to Information Act, 2005

Muslim Personal law (Shariat) Application Act 1937

JUDGMENTS OF THE COURT:

Shakti Vahini vs. Union of India & Ors. [2018] 3 SCR 770 : (2018) 7 SCC 192

Citation: WRIT PETITION (CIVIL) NO. 231 OF 2010

Vineeta Sharma Vs Rakesh Sharma (2020) 9 SCC 1DECIDED ON : 11 August 2020

Judgment on triple talak - Shayara Bano v. Union of India & Others, Writ Petition (C) No. 118 of 2016

Mohini Jain v. State of Karnataka 1992 AIR 1858

Unni Krishnan, J.P & Ors. v. State of Andhra Pradesh & Ors. 1993 AIR 217

Avinash Mehrotra v. Union of India 6 SCC 398 (2009)

Vellore Citizens Welfare Forum vs Union Of India & Ors on 28 August, 1996, AIR 1996 SC 2715: (1996) 5 SCC 647

www.ingramcontent.com/pod-product-compliance
Ingram Content Group UK Ltd.
Pitfield, Milton Keynes, MK11 3LW, UK
UKHW062259290726
14090UKWH00017B/776